To my Now Good Friend
Andy —

Now you know "Y"!

Z

Your Friend

Steve

TRAINED BY A HOUND DOG

An Acclaimed Hunter's True-Life Story

By
Ed Vance

Trained by a Hound Dog
An Acclaimed Hunter's True-Life Story

Copyright 2018 by Ed Vance

Print ISBN: 979-8-88589-373-2

2nd Edition (February 24th, 2022)

Cover photo copyright 1972 by Midge Dandridge

Used by permission by Midge Dandridge

Images copyright Ed Vance, Midge Dandridge, Jim Dougherty.

Photos of Charlie Tant unknown owner

Howard Bilton Photo's provided by Dan Johnson

Published in the United States of America.

Printed in the United States. All rights reserved under International Copyright Law.

Cover and/or contents may not be reproduced in any manner without the express written permission of the author.

All stories contained in this book are the author's remembrances and thoughts and has been written solely by the author.

TRAINED BY A HOUND DOG

An Acclaimed Hunter's True-Life Story

ED VANCE, an acclaimed hunter, was one of the few hunters who made his living by hunting only for mountain lions and bears in the mountains and forests of California, Idaho, Nevada, Utah, and Montana for 25 years. Featured in Bowhunters Digest 1st. edition, Los Angeles Times West Magazine (1967), Saga Magazine (1968), Western Outdoors (1968), Bow & Arrow Magazine (1971), Bow & Arrow Magazine (1973), Western Outdoors News (1968-1973), and more currently Bear Hunting Magazine September/October (2019). Ed Vance risked everything to follow his dreams, and without knowing it, chiseled a name for himself and for his dogs in the history of these places. The bond between the hunter and his hounds was one of deep trust and reliance, in a time when the changing landscape threatened to take it all. *Trained by a Hound Dog* recounts the legends of the hunt, in the authentic voice of the man who was there, told as if the reader were sitting with him around a campfire. The true stories he tells of his hounds and the lions and bears they caught in some of the country's toughest terrain and conditions are a glimpse into an era of Western History that has faded from view.

"The old time way of hunting and peoples' views of country living was changing. Like it or not, it was coming. The old lion hunters that once roamed these hills, hunters like Jay Bruce, Charlie Leadshaw, or Howard Bilton, and others are now gone. All that's left of this, is knowing there was a time when they were here, and at that time there was only one way to get it done, and that was the hard way. Today they are only a part of history, a history that unfortunately cannot be duplicated."

— ED VANCE, *TRAINED BY A HOUND DOG*

ACKNOWLEDGEMENTS

I want to thank my wife, LYNETTE, because without her encouragement this book would never have been written. Also, I want to thank, GARY BRIDGES, ROY STEPHENSON, JOE BRYAN, LOUIS STRAWN, BERGIN RIDDLE, GARY and MARY ANN GRENFELL for their help, and MISS T.K. RICHARDSON for all of her work.

DEDICATION

1966
Myself with Bo

Once I had all the wrong ways figured out and realized that I knew nothing about hunting, I got lucky. I purchased a six-year-old Redtick Hound who was born in Arkansas and then at the age of two, was moved to California. He was best known as a small game dog that had caught a ton of bobcats, foxes and raccoons. He had never caught a lion or a bear on his own, and for that matter, neither had I. But things were about to change for both of us. He became my mentor. I CALLED HIM BO.

TABLE OF CONTENTS

ACKNOWLEDGEMENTS	IX
DEDICATION	XI

PART I

THE BEGINNING	3
BO & PAT-II	25
RUBE CREEK	29
DEAD MULE SADDLE	39
SAYLOR	45
GLENNVILLE	53
PEEL MILL CREEK	75
THE RINCON TRAIL	85
JOHNSONDALE	93
TELEPHONE RIDGE	105
CHANGING LANDSCAPE	115
NORTHERN CALIFORNIA	125
IRON CREEK	135
FROM DEVIL'S KITCHEN TO BULL RUN	149
MOUNTAIN LIONS & POLITICIANS	171
NEVADA AND UTAH	181
MONTANA	205
BEAR HUNTING IN IDAHO	229

PART II

BITS & PIECES	235
LAST CHAPTER	265
ABOUT THE AUTHOR	267

1967
Sandy Creek
Kern County, California

PART I

Chapter 1

THE BEGINNING

Did you ever feel like you were born at the wrong time or in the wrong place? Well, if you did then you weren't alone. As far back as I could remember I wanted to live in the country, maybe on a farm, own some type of domestic animals and at least have a chance to hunt for wild animals. However, growing up in the suburbs of southern California didn't offer many opportunities to do anything like that. Yeah, as an eight year old I had fun heading out into those brush-covered hills around Glendale California, carrying my Daisy Red Ryder BB gun with me, and make believing that this was hunting, only it wasn't, and down deep inside, I knew that. At the time I never thought that the day would come when I would get my chance at the real thing.

It wasn't until I was nineteen years old that my life started to change. At the time I was working in Van Nuys, California at the General Motors Chevrolet assembly plant. I was on the assembly lines installing various parts onto the 1960 passenger cars and pickup trucks. Here I am, working the night shift that ran from 3:30 p.m. to 12 a.m., five days a week, when I met a guy working opposite from me who was from Georgia. He said he was a Mormon, and he wanted to move to Salt Lake City, Utah, only he needed to earn and save as much money as he could before leaving Van Nuys. Like myself, he just needed a job, any job, so here I am. We would visit with each other only when time would allow, which wasn't very often. The assembly line that we were working on was moving at the rate of fifty cars per hour, and sometimes even faster. With only one minute or less per car to get our job done and move onto the next one, needless to say, there was little time to visit.

When we were able to get around to it, he said he didn't care much for California, and that he kind of missed Georgia, but he needed to get to Salt Lake City. He went on to explain that he had lived on a farm and that he and his friends hunted there. This captured my attention, farm life and hunting, all in one package—I was all ears. Then one night he mentioned that he used to go coon hunting with his friends in the Okefenokee swamps of Georgia using hounds, and his stories were always interesting, some even exciting, and it wasn't long before I was hooked, I wanted to know more. I had never heard of this type of hunting before, but it sure caught my attention. Now keep in mind, I knew nothing about hounds, where to buy one, where to go to hunt them, or how to hunt them. In fact, I had never even heard of this before; I was as green as it gets. The only thing that I knew for sure was that I didn't belong in Los Angeles and wanted out of the big city. My goal was to do everything I could dream of to change that.

It didn't take long until this guy suggested I take a look into some of the major hunting magazines. Just go to the back pages he said, and you will see ads where these dogs are for sale. Well, I got a bunch of these magazines, and it didn't take long before I was writing letters, asking these sellers what hounds they had for sale. He liked Blueticks the best, but said that Redbones, Black and Tans, and Walkers were all just as good. It was all just a matter of choice, and within six months I had myself a Redbone hound. I purchased him from a kennel in Arkansas, had him placed in a wooden crate and sent to me by railroad. I think I paid thirty-five dollars for him, and the shipping was about the same.

1960
My first hunting hound, Buck

The railroad trip took about ten days, and when he arrived, we made friends in no time at all. His name was Buck, not a bad looking hound, minded fine, knew his name, looked to be about four-years-old and someone even had his ears tattooed, a practice used by some of the better houndsmen for various reasons of personal identification. I liked him right away. Then my friend on the assembly line told me that I really would do better if I had two dogs, so now I'm on a search for a second dog. My wife at the time had relatives that owned a farm in the Fresno area and while on a trip to see them I was directed to a local hunter there who sold me a young Redbone female named Minnie. Alright, now I'm ready. Now all I had to do was find a place to go hunting. I had lived in Ventura before moving to Van Nuys, and I knew that the mountains around there were supposed to have deer and mountain lions, so that looked like a good place to start. I had no experience of any hunting there, but I needed to get out of the Los Angeles area, so I quit General Motors and moved to Ojai, California.

My wife that was about a year younger than I was and we had two children that were one and two years old, so we needed a place for the four of us. It didn't take long, and I found a little farmhouse on the outskirts of town where I could have dogs, and it also had provisions for horse's, which

I immediately bought two. Then, I got a job working in a self-service gas station in Santa Paula, worked ten to twelve hours a day, six days a week. It didn't take long, and I made friends with a couple of older guys who had hounds, and they invited me to hunt with them. They talked a good story, and the dogs ran something every time we went hunting, only we never caught anything. After a few months of this, I started to get suspicious, and I doubted that they were actually chasing anything that could climb a tree.

We hunted at night during the working week and every day that I had off I would head for the woods as well. It made no difference, no matter who I was hunting with, the outcome was always the same. We got into long, hard races every time we went out, but we never caught anything. After about a year of this and hearing all sorts of excuses from these guys, I decided that I needed to quit hunting with them, and I started looking elsewhere to hunt.

By now my wife was fed up with me, couldn't take the strain of my working and hunting as much as I did, so she divorced me and took the kids to San Francisco to live with her mother. This was not exactly what I wanted, but to her the damage was done and she was out of here. So now it was just me with a couple of dogs that couldn't catch anything and a job that I still had to work at from sixty to seventy hours a week to cover my expenses. I quit my job at the gas station, and I got into working on housing tracts as a carpenter in the area. After joining the carpenters' union I started making pretty good money, and unlike the gas stations, these jobs were only eight hours a day, five days a week.

Eventually, I figured that I needed a good, proven dog, one that had been properly trained, had been hunting in my part of the world, or somewhere similar to this, and had caught both bobcats and lions. At the very least, it needed to have hunted under similar conditions. When I bought Buck, he was supposed to be a trained coon dog, and he might have been just that, but that's not what I was trying to catch. The other dogs that I had exposed him to when hunting with these other hunters were obviously not trained dogs at all. They simply would run anything that got out in front of them and that was usually a deer. I had a hard time convincing any of these guys that I had been hunting with, that they were only fooling themselves into believing that if we all had faster dogs we would start treeing bobcats, raccoons, and the like. This was not the way I came to see it, and in my opinion, all we had now was a bunch of dogs that went looking for deer to run as soon as they hit the ground.

    I came to the conclusion that the only thing I could do now was to start over, and that meant new hunting friends, new dogs and a different place to hunt. I found a good home for Buck and Minnie, let them go to some new owners who didn't hunt and really liked them. Now I was suddenly without dogs, and ready to start all over again. Then I met another carpenter who had lived in Utah, and he told me about a government hunter there named Willis Butolph, who had actually caught more lions than I ever thought possible. He told me how to contact him and I took a chance and wrote him a letter, asking if I could come and see him. I told him what I had been trying to do, and asked if he would be interested in selling any of his dogs. Much to my surprise he wrote back, and said that he had only one that he would consider selling. He was a redbone and the only reason he would sell him was that he wouldn't run a bear. He invited me to come and hunt with him. He gave me the directions to where he lived, and I was on my way. It was only about 700 miles from where I lived to this guy's house and if I could get what I wanted and needed, 700 miles wasn't that far away. So, I jumped into my old beat up 1951 GMC three quarter ton pickup and hit the road. I had never been to Utah and I was surprised to see so many animals along the highways in that state.

    It was now October 1962, and late in the evening by the time I arrived at Willis' house. There were dogs tied up all over the place; most of them were Plotts, one Bluetick and another a Black and Tan. None of them got up to see who I was as I pulled in, and they all appeared to be tired, and more interested in sleeping. Willis lived in a very typical, small type of farmhouse that was probably built in the 1920s. He met me at the front door, welcomed me in right away and introduced me to his wife, Myrtle, who was also very friendly. It was early fall and I didn't have much time to spend with him because I had only taken about a week off from work, and I would be spending two to three of those days on the road, which didn't leave much time to do anything else. But this trip was important to me and I had good feelings about it. As soon as I got there we both started talking about hunting. He wanted to know what I knew, which was very little, and I wanted to get to know him and learn as much as possible in the short time I had to spend with him.

We had been visiting for about two hours or so when I asked him how long it had been since he caught any lions. He paused for a moment and appeared as though he was trying to remember back in time. Then he said, "Today." In fact, it had been only a few hours since he had finished skinning it out. What a surprise! I could hardly believe it; here we had been talking for over two hours and this guy acted like he had forgot all about killing a lion only a few hours earlier. I asked him what he had done with it, and he took me to his back porch and showed me the freshly skinned lion hide, tacked and salted down to the wooden floor of his back porch. I was impressed. For the first time in my life, I felt that I was in the right place.

It was sometime during the night that he received a phone call from a sheep rancher who said that a lion had killed a bunch of his sheep the night before at one of his camps over in the Book Cliffs Mountains, and needed his help. He asked if I wanted to go with him and I jumped at the chance. We would be leaving early the next morning, and since I would be needing a horse for the hunt, Willis asked if the rancher could supply me with one, which he gladly agreed to do.

It was only about a forty-five minute drive from Willis' house to where we were to meet with a couple of sheepherders at an old corral, in the mouth of a canyon. This led to the area where this lion had killed these sheep, and as promised, the herders were there, along with a horse for me. As I was saddling up, adjusting my stirrups, and tightening the cinch, I couldn't help but notice that Willis was paying particular attention to how I was doing things. When I finished, he walked over, lifted up the stirrups on each side to see what I had done, glanced over at me and with a slight smile on his face he said, "I'm surprised." He clearly hadn't expected that I knew the proper way to saddle a horse. I just smiled back and mounted up. No doubt about it, I wasn't a well seasoned cowboy or anything like that, but I had owned a few horses, had my share of saddle sores and knew the proper way to get it done. From there Willis led the way as we headed out together to see what had happened.

It was about eight in the morning when Willis and I along with five hounds, rode into the sheep camp, high in the Book Cliffs Mountains of Utah, and that was where I met and stayed with Pete, a migrant sheepherder from Mexico. It was easy to see that he was totally relieved to see us. We spent about thirty minutes talking with him and looking the area over to see what this lion had done. Pete and another sheepherder had just finished moving his tent about 500 feet away from where it was the night before which was completely surrounded with dead sheep. I guessed that moving his camp was easier than dragging all the carcasses away. The three of us walked over to look at the old site where these dead sheep were, and there it was, just as Pete said. One of them was less than thirty feet from the front of where his tent had been sitting with about another dozen or so scattered all around within a hundred feet of that. As I recall, he had three sheepdogs who had tried to run the lion off, but the lion chased them all back into his tent with him, where all he had was an oil lantern that didn't cast light much further than twenty feet.

Pete said it seemed like it lasted for hours, but in reality he said it probably didn't take that long, from start to finish—maybe only five to ten minutes Then the lion simply walked away without eating a thing. Pete had been terrified to the bone and neither he nor his dogs came out of the tent until the sun came up in the morning. It was only then that he could see what had actually happened. During the attack, Pete's only horse, which was hobbled at the time, ran off, hobbles and all, looking for safety and leaving Pete without anything to ride out of there. The next closest sheep camp was about five miles away, so he walked as fast as he could to get help. Needless to say, Pete was scared out of his wits, which was understandable if you put yourself into his position of being alone in the middle of the night with the only thing between you and this killing spree was your tent wall, which was just a thin piece of canvas. When he got to the next camp, he told the whole story to the other sheepherders who then relayed this information to the owner and rancher who called Willis for help. All of this took quite a while and in the meantime, the trail was getting colder, giving the lion an easy getaway.

After talking with Pete, Willis and I rode out and cut a large circle around the area to see if the dogs could pick up any sign of the lion. Because so much time had passed, the dogs were unable to pick up a trail, so we returned to camp, figuring we could wait until the next day and see if it returned.

Willis then decided it would be best if he rode to check on another sheep camp that was only a few miles away to see if this lion might have showed up there, leaving me to stay with Pete. He left me with three of his dogs to hunt with, Pat, who was one of his best dogs, Red, the dog he was willing to sell, and another Plott hound, and some simple instructions for where to go and how to handle them. He told me he would be back in two days and wanted me to stay there and hunt for this lion. This all came to me as quite a surprise, since I had never caught a lion in my life, didn't know his dogs, and definitely didn't know the country. Regardless, he seemed to trust me and I was going to give it a try. I stayed as instructed and hunted all around the area with Willis' dogs, but there was no sign of the lion.

At camp the first night, Pete and I shared some of our experiences; he spoke English very well and was an interesting man. He told me how he would travel from his home to Utah, where he would spend two full years watching over another man's sheep. The rancher supplied Pete with everything he needed to survive his primitive lifestyle, tobacco and all by opening up a savings account in the nearby town of Price, where he deposited Pete's payment each month. So Pete never saw any money until it was time for him to head back to Mexico, and since he had no expenses he could save every penny he earned, which as I recall, was about $1,200 a year. At the end of his two-year contract, he would withdraw all his money and buy a round trip bus ticket to Mexico. Once he got there, he would immediately get married to someone who stayed with him until all of his money was gone, which usually took less than a month. Then he would turn around and head back to Utah for another two years. He went on to say that every time he did this, his wife at the time would divorce him while he was gone, and that opened the door for him to marry another woman when he went back to Mexico.

This guy went wherever the sheep went, and it made no difference how hot or cold it was, he would stay with them. During the winter months he would move them to the lower elevations and onto the valley floor where he was given a trailer that was specially designed for the occasion. Otherwise, when he was up in the higher mountains during the warmer months, he lived in a tent. Most of the time, he was alone except for his dogs, the sheep, the rancher who would bring him supplies, and an occasional visitor, which was usually another sheepherder, or hunter, like Willis or myself. It was easy to tell he was living a very lonely life, but someone had to do it and he seemed to like it.

I must admit that I enjoyed my time with Pete, but after two days of hunting and with no sign of the lion's return, I felt the need to get going and see what happened to Willis. It was easy to see the disappointment in Pete's eyes when I told him I was leaving. Before I left, I asked Pete if I could take a photo of him. He was very willing and asked if I could give him a few minutes to get ready. I was totally surprised and had no idea what he had in mind when he went into his tent.

When he came out he was really dressed for the occasion. He had put on his best hat, chaps with attached ammo pocket that could hold a box of .30-30 cartridges, a wool-lined denim jacket along with his Winchester lever action rifle. He asked if it would be all right for him to call in two of his dogs for the photo event. He seemed honored that someone wanted to take a photo of him, and of course I agreed. Pete was a very nice man and also an excellent campfire cook. Although that was the one and only time I ever saw him, I never forgot our time together.

Mexican Pete, all dressed up in his finest.

I never asked for his last name or how old he was; I thought he was somewhere in his 40's. It was hard to tell, since his was a hard life, and most sheepherders looked older than they actually were.

It was time for me to go. I was saddled up with my sleeping gear on the back of the saddle, I kept two dogs snapped together and I let Pat loose to hunt on the way out. From here I rode back to where I was given the horse, cleaned him off, put him back in the same corral that I found him in and was off.

This is a typical sight when visiting most sheep camps. They were rough and placed just about anywhere there was an opening and water close by. That's all it took and there they were.

The dogs in this photo from left to right. Pat is the Plott hound with his back to the camera. This is the Pat dog that I purchased from Willis a few years after I met Pete. Next is Red, a Redbone hound that I purchased around the time of the lion attack on Pete's camp. The other dog to the far right was also a Plott, but I forgot his name.

Since Willis hadn't shown back up at Pete's camp as expected, I headed back to his house and found him setting next to his telephone. He immediately asked me what had happened at Pete's and I responded by asking, "Why didn't you come back?" He said that there wasn't any lion trouble at the other camp so he headed for home and was planning to come back to Pete's camp later but thought he would stick around home an extra day and sit by his phone. He said that during the summer months he could catch more lions just by answering phone calls than he could riding out in the hills looking for them. What he meant by this was, with the sheep in the higher country during these months where they grazed in prime lion country, there were more sheep getting killed on a regular basis. That made finding them easier as long as the sheepherders called him before the tracks of the lion or in some cases, bear, got too old for the dogs to trail. Most of the time, the only ones that got caught were the lions that stayed close by for a day or two. At the time, I didn't understand this, but in time I learned that finding a lion was usually the hardest part of catching them.

Before leaving, I purchased a Redbone named Red, and he was actually a pretty good, well-trained dog with a lot of experience catching lions and bobcats. The only reason for selling Red to me was that he would not run a bear and that didn't fit into Willis' pack of dogs too well. For me, this was a good deal. I had met someone who had good dogs, had caught an unbelievable amount of lions, I had an eye opening experience, and I finally owned the kind of dog that I needed.

I checked with Willis a few months later to see if the lion ever went back to Pete's camp and it had not. Some lions are funny that way. They would go in, kill a bunch of sheep without eating any of them and be on their way. This type of activity was more the exception than the rule with lions in that area. Then one day while on another visit to see Willis, we went into a café in Price, Utah, he told me that the largest number of sheep that he had seen killed in a single event was by one female lion who killed 130 sheep, give or take a few. Every one of them was found dead in a *sleeping* position. The lion appeared to have come from behind and bit each one on the back of the neck, killing it instantly. There was no fighting or struggling; she just killed them and went on her way. Willis eventually caught this lion. She was young, average in size (105 to110 pounds) and it was estimated that she had killed well over 300 sheep in her lifetime. After telling me this story, he asked if I believed him. I thought it was probably a loaded question so I said, well, I guess so. There was another older man sitting with us at the time and he asked him the same question. He looked at Willis and told him, of course I do, all those sheep were mine. That's just the way it was: Willis always had something up his sleeve.

Below is Red, the Redbone that I purchased from Willis Butolph. I later sold him to my friend Bergin Riddle, who kept him until the good hound passed away.

Red was no doubt the first well-trained dog that I ever had. The only fault with him was that he would not run a bear.

Not long after I bought Red from Willis, my ex-wife and I decided to patch things up and make another go at it, so I sold Red to a friend of mine in California, Bergin Riddle, who was a Government trapper. But this time things between us was worst than the first time, so within only a few months I was single again and with no dogs. Here I go again, looking for a hunting hound. First, I contacted Bergin to see if he would sell Red back to me, but no luck there, Red was working out real good for him, and he kept him for the rest of his life. So, I called Willis to see if he had anything that he would let go and the only thing that he would consider selling was a young Plott that he named Rebel. He had been on several lion hunts and did okay, but didn't like bears, so like Red he was not what Willis wanted.

Willis' friend, Olin Greer, who lived in Gillett, Wyoming originally trained Rebel. Olin hunted there for bobcats and raccoons, which was very good training for young dogs. So, I bought Rebel and he was looking like he was going to work out. Then I located a Black and Tan hound that I ended up purchasing from a guy in Texas. He was trained to hunt coons and bobcats as well. He was good looking, well trained, and I felt he might be what I needed to go along with Rebel. His name was Slim. I caught a few raccoons with these two within a short time of putting them together, but it was lions that I really wanted. Then, while I was lion hunting in the Sespe Creek Area of Ventura County, I ran into Ted Hasting and Calvin Fields, two well-known lion hunters. I was anxious to hunt with them because I knew that they had both caught quite a few lions in their lifetime.

It was November 1963, conditions were very dry and the days were hot, so trailing was not going to be easy for the dogs. The scent was faint, but we could see tracks fairly well in the dusty trails. In the late morning hours we found where a lion had recently crossed a firebreak and its tracks were fresh enough for the dogs to trail. Between the three of us there must have been about eight or nine dogs after this lion and it wasn't long before they had it treed. I could hardly believe it. I was finally looking up a tree at a real lion and my dogs were there, treeing it.

The California bounty for lions had been eliminated only weeks before, but that made no difference; we were all in for shooting it, and Ted was the one that was going to do it. It didn't matter to me who did the shooting. I was just thrilled to be involved, and have my two dogs there. This lion was only about fifteen feet up in a small pine tree that was surrounded with heavy, thick brush that was almost as tall as the tree itself. This made it difficult to gather up any of the dogs before Ted took a shot. The last thing we wanted was to have a wounded lion on the ground, especially with any of the dogs loose.

Ted thought the lion was going to jump when it first saw us, so before we could catch any of the dogs and tie them back and away from the tree that the lion was in, he took his shot, literally blowing it out of the tree. As soon as the lion hit the ground there were dogs all over it and every one of them got a mouth full of fur. Not knowing whether the first shot had killed it, Ted cycled another round into his .30-30 Winchester and fired again. Only this time, his second shot went completely through the lion and hit my dog Slim in his muzzle, blowing most of his upper teeth out on his right side of his mouth. It didn't kill him, but he was definitely in need of immediate medical attention.

I wasted no time getting Slim out of the woods and to a Veterinarian Hospital in Ojai, about an hour drive away. He was rushed in ahead of the other patients and straight into surgery. This vet was a very good doctor and although he saved his life, Slims' days as a hunting dog were over. He had to have multiple surgeries before he was completely healed up, and eventually I found someone who liked him and kept him as a pet. So, I was back to just one dog, Rebel.

You might say that the hunt came as a double-edged sword: we caught a lion, which was my first, but I lost a dog that I really liked in the process. What happened was no doubt an accident, I was sure of that, but it was also a grim lesson for all of us when it comes to shooting a high-powered rifle into an area where others could be injured or killed. I had been hunting for only three years and had gone through several dogs that didn't make the grade and now I lost Slim. Being of a hardheaded nature to begin with, there was no way I was giving up. I was single, made a reasonable amount of money working as a carpenter and I was willing to spend every penny to get what I wanted, and that was a good dog.

I called Willis again to see if I could visit and do some hunting with him. It was winter and there would be snow all over the State of Utah, which made it much easier to find and catch lions than it was where I lived in Southern California, where it is all bare-ground trailing. I loaded up Rebel and headed for Utah and as expected, it was cold, with plenty of snow. It looked like the hunting would be good with the conditions the way they were. I arrived at Willis' house in the late afternoon, spent the night there, and early in the morning we headed out on a hunt.

Within two hours we caught a male lion that had just killed a four point mule deer. This kill was so fresh that the deer was still warm; the lion had barely enough time to open it up before we came along. The lion was treed in a very small fir tree and only about twenty feet above the ground, making it easy to get the noose around his neck without having to climb up the tree. But as we pulled it out it lost his balance and came down headfirst, killing it instantly. This came as a total surprise to us, but I was learning that these lions might not be as tough as one would think. From there we went on hunting for a few more hours before we called it a day.

When we returned to Willis' home we learned that his father had just died. The funeral was to be held in a couple of days, so I volunteered to drive him to Wyoming, where his father had been living. He accepted my offer and that same night we left on a 700-mile trip to Sundance in a blowing snowstorm. At the time I had a new International Scout 4X4 truck, and on this drive we learned that those trucks were not very well thought-out when it came to heaters. With the heater going full blast, we still had to wrap ourselves in blankets most of the time, just to keep warm, but it got us there and back.

The trip turned out to be quite an education. For the next four days I had the opportunity to visit with a man who was truly a living legend when it came to government lion hunting. We talked about hunting all the way there and back, and I was impressed to learn that at the time he had about 450 documented lion kills. He told me that when he was a small child, he and his parents migrated from Missouri to Sundance in a covered wagon, where they built a sod house on their homestead. It was hard for me to believe, but here I was, driving down a paved road in a four-wheel drive truck with a radio, a "heater," all the comforts of highway travel, and next to me was a legendary lion and bear hunter who started his life in a house with no plumbing, a dirt floor, and to go somewhere, you walked or used a horse to get there. Needless to say, I was all ears. What a story!

But then, on our way back it came time to talk about my real reason for being there, and it wasn't just to hunt with Willis. I had something much more important in mind: I was also there to see if I could buy another dog from him, and this time I wanted to get one of his lead dogs. I knew it might not be at all possible, but I was going to give it a try. Before I left home, I had gone to the bank and took out a loan for a thousand dollars. It was all that I could afford, and I didn't know if this would be enough to do the trick, but it was worth a try.

We were about half way back from Wyoming when I told him that I was in the market for buying another dog and asked him about the possibility of him selling Pat. I mentioned that everyone I had talked to who knew Pat thought he was his best bare-ground lion dog, but it was common knowledge that Pat would not run a bear at all. Since Willis hunted bears as well, I was hoping this would help to convince him to sell me this dog. At the time I didn't care about bears so that part didn't bother me. All I wanted to catch was lions and I was determined to do that. I also realized it wasn't that likely for a full-time professional hunter to give up one of his best dogs for any amount of money. That might have been the case with him, but I was going to find out.

At first he didn't want to talk about it and I could understand why. Pat was only five years old and in his prime. Plus, he was supposed to be an outstanding lion hound in either snow, dry, or bare ground. Everything that I had heard about him was that he got it done and he didn't need any help doing it. I wanted to put him with Rebel, who was still my only other dog. I knew this would work for me and was really hoping he would go for it. I started off with an offer of six hundred dollars, but it didn't faze him at all. So I waited for about an hour or so. We talked about this and that and then my offer went up to seven hundred. Again, he didn't seem to be interested. Then, after about another hour or so, I upped it to eight hundred, then nine hundred, and finally I had his attention. When I hit $1,000, he caved in. I couldn't believe it. He said yes.

It was hard to believe, but I now owned a first-class lion hound—Pat was mine. I could hardly wait to return to Willis' house and head out on a hunt. When we got back, the snow was good, the sun came out and off we went. I parked my Scout and started a walk up the base of a canyon looking for tracks. Willis was to meet me a mile or so at another road where he would give me a ride back to my truck. I wanted to let my two dogs hunt loose out in front of me for a little while. I didn't need to do it this way since I was in fresh snow and I'd be able to see any lion tracks, but that's what I wanted to do.

So, I let these two loose to hunt on their own. We walked up the canyon as planned, and found the road where I was to meet Willis. My dogs were only a short distance ahead of me when disaster hit. Along the side of the road and in plain sight, there was a warning sign that no dog hunter wants to see: It read, "Beware! Poison Bait in This Area!" I immediately started calling for Pat and Rebel as I ran along their tracks. Within seconds I saw them both trying to eat this frozen sheep leg. It was about zero degrees out and it was so hard that it didn't look as though they were able to get any of the meat. But I couldn't be sure. At the same time Willis showed up and we loaded both of them into his truck, and headed for town as fast as we could go.

We were over an hour drive away from the nearest veterinarian's office. I called the vet as soon as we had arrived at Willis' home and the doctor told us that all they needed to do was lick it and it would be enough to kill them. He went on to say that we could do both of these dogs a favor if we shot and killed them before the poison started in on them. He was right; they had gotten enough. It hit Pat first and then about fifteen minutes later it hit Rebel. 1080 poison; it's tasteless, odorless, colorless, has no antidote, and it can kill again if anything should eat part of the first victim. In 1972, this poison was banned for use on all federal land in the United States. But since it works so "well," people have figured out ways to get around the ban, and as recent as 2016 there have been reports of its illegal use in some parts of the country. Those still using it probably don't care, but for anyone else who wants to know, its victims don't just lie down and go to sleep after eating it— far from it. It took about thirty minutes of agonizing pain to kill Pat who died first and as I watched Rebel going through the same torture Pat had just gone through, I did what the vet suggested and shot Rebel. What I saw should turn anyone's stomach and I, like many others, believe that it should never have been made legal in the first place. The stuff is so deadly that quantities less than one five-hundredth of an ounce will kill a dog and one teaspoonful would kill a hundred people.

I was devastated, and with this loss I felt totally defeated and I didn't know what to do except to head for home. So I tucked my tail between my legs and left, only this time without any dogs. It didn't take all that long for me to realize that I still wasn't going to give up. I wanted this more than ever before. So I licked my wounds as best I could, and set out to start all over again.

It was now 1964, and I was still working as a carpenter, framing tract houses in Thousand Oaks, California, and I had injured my back to the point that I was going to have to stop, at least the framing part of it. By then I had bought several dogs that I thought could do the job, yet was having little to no success. It was obvious that I was in a part of California that was just not cut out for hound hunting. This made no difference to me, in fact I was more determined than ever. However, I really had no idea of where to look next. I had given up hunting with some locals I knew, the same guys I repeatedly had no success with.

Then I learned of an older gentleman by the name of J.D. Reynolds who had a six-year-old Redtick hound that he might be interested in selling. He lived on a farm outside of Wasco, California, so I called him to see if what I heard was correct and if I could come hunt with him, and find out what this dog could do. We set up a date for the next weekend to meet at a place in the Greenhorn Mountains called Jack Ranch. I knew the place and had hunted there a few times, but not on any private land. The area is adjacent to the Sequoia National Forest and was an area that I had come to like very much.

Then on this hunt, J.D. told me that he wanted four hundred dollars for the dog and was firm on that price. He was a very good looking dog, weighed about fifty-five pounds. They called him Bo. J.D. brought along two other dogs of his own, and his friend Roy, who had another dog, for a total of four dogs. It was March, and the grass was up to where the trailing was good. It was about 9 p.m., when J.D. and Roy turned their dogs loose. They said that all four of them had been broken of running deer and coyotes, and were very reliable small game dogs, but none of these had ever been on any lions or bears.

J.D. and Roy turned their dogs loose at the same time and it took only about ten minutes when one of them struck a trail, and it was Bo. Bo trailed for about a quarter mile before any of the others put in with him. Then the race was on, with all four dogs running wide open, and after a chase that lasted for only a few minutes it was suddenly over! J.D. said right off that Bo was treed, and one by one the others joined in with him. Not knowing one dog's voice from another, I could only take his word for it, but it was easy to see that only one in this bunch was leading the way, and they both agreed that it was Bo. Roy didn't seem too happy to admit it, and I was thinking it sure looked as though Bo had really done this by himself since the other dogs were all behind him from start to finish. When we got to the tree we found that high in a black oak, there was a good-sized bobcat. J. D. came from the old school that preached that it was important to kill everything that the dogs treed, so he shot it out, and we were on our way looking for another one.

From there we went just a little further before Bo struck another track; the same thing happened as before, only this time it was a fox that he had treed ahead of the other dogs. Though it's not common elsewhere, the cross foxes in that part of the country will climb a tree if the dogs put enough pressure on them. I was totally surprised by Bo's abilities, and I honestly didn't expect to see this dog do so well. Because of this, I didn't bring enough money with me to buy him, or I would have bought him right on the spot. By now it was getting late and I needed to head back home, so I asked if I could come back the next weekend and told him that if Bo could do anything like this again, I would buy him.

Before heading home, I had to ask J.D. why he was selling him, and he made it very simple: He liked to train dogs as much as he liked hunting them, and at six, Bo was getting up in years. He thought it would be best to find him a new owner before he got too old to sell. I thought, "Too old?" Well, he wasn't too old for me, and when I returned the next weekend Bo did it all over again, only this time it was two bobcats. So I didn't hesitate. I bought him and headed for home.

In the years that followed I would learn that to call Bo "good" was an understatement. Was he perfect? No. But as far as hunting dogs go, he was outstanding in every way. From that day on I began hunting as much as I could with Bo and he proved, over and over again that he really didn't need any help from me or other dogs. If he caught the scent of something, he almost always treed it. I always had a hard time believing that J.D. sold this dog to me, and I was sure that there were times when he regretted it as well—he was everything I wanted and then some. Finally, after a very rough road, it looked like things were changing for the better, and with the help of this one dog, I was starting to learn what hound hunting was about. This old Redtick hound dog was the one that was going to show me the way. Believe it or not, I was about to be trained by a hound dog.

Chapter 2

BO & PAT-II

For nearly four years I had struggled to learn how to make it all work. I had purchased about ten dogs, paid hundreds in vet bills, resold one, gave away most of the others, and ruined several by putting them into the wrong company from my own lack of knowledge. Not to mention the pain of watching two die from 1080 poison.

All that time, I had seen only a small handful of animals put up a tree, and now standing with me was a dog that caught something nearly every time his feet hit the ground. Having all the bad experiences in the past, I must admit that when I first started to hunt with Bo I was quite nervous about letting him get out of my sight for fear of losing him, but that's not the way it works, I knew that if I was going to hunt with trail hounds, I had to let them go and do it on their own, so that's what I did.

Within two months of acquiring Bo, I called Willis, told him what I now had with Bo. I asked if he could help me to find a young dog to go with Bo. He mentioned that he had acquired a son of Pat, the dog that I lost with Rebel to the 1080 poison. He was just turning two years old, and looked to him like he might make a pretty good dog in time. Pat II had been started on bobcats in Wyoming by Willis' friend, Olin Greer, who Willis had used many times to get young dogs up and going. He looked just like his dad, and because of that they called him Pat-II. Due to what had happened with his dad and Rebel, Willis offered to sell him to me for two hundred dollars, if I would come and get him. So, I was on my way back to Utah to get a partner for Bo. After picking up Pat-II we headed right back home.

It was easy to see that Pat II needed more hunting experience, but he was no trouble, had no bad habits, stuck real close to Bo, and the two got along just fine. I couldn't expect to use him as a start dog, but he had been on a few lions, where Bo had not.

I was still working fulltime in the summer months as a carpenter in Thousand Oaks, and only part-time for the balance of the year. Every Friday after work, I would go home, clean up, load my two dogs and head out for a place to hunt. My favorite spot was a four-hour drive each way to the Greenhorn Mountains in the Sierras, where Bo was trained.

In August, we made a quick trip to Paris, Texas to hunt with the same guy who sold me Slim; who said he had a male Black and Tan that he thought I would like. He was probably an okay dog, but I didn't see what I was looking for in him, so after we did some hunting, we returned to California without buying anything.

As we passed through the town of Needles, California, on our way back, it was late afternoon and blazing hot, I think around 120 degrees. At the time, I was driving the same 1963 International Scout that I had when Willis and I went to Wyoming, and it did not have any air conditioning. Bo and Pat-II were so hot, and panting so hard they could barely breath. The only form of air conditioning I had was to open all the windows and keep moving. So in an attempt to cool them down I pulled into a gas station, bought a large bag of ice, and broke it open and they both started eating it as fast as they could. Within minutes they were both asleep, pumped full of ice and doing well. They slept all the way to where we were living back in Ventura.

Although I came home sort of empty-handed, I didn't feel the trip was a waste of time because I did get to meet and hunt with other hound hunters. One was a FBI agent whose job it was to hunt down and destroy whisky stills in Oklahoma and Texas. I thought that was really interesting. I got to hunt with a couple of nice guys, who had some pretty decent dogs. I was having no trouble catching bobcats, raccoons, and foxes. I just couldn't get Bo to trail a lion. I had tried Bo several times on what I thought were fairly fresh lion tracks, but he just wouldn't pay any attention to them.

Then on an early November morning while I was hunting on the Sandy Creek Fire Road, Pat II found something that he couldn't let go of. His tail was up and wagging and nose on it. So far, Pat II had never run anything wrong, and it was always Bo who started the track first. But this time was different, Pat-II found something, and he was all fired up, he was trying to trail something that Bo had no interest in. As fast as I could go, I started looking around to see what Pat II was trying to trail, and there it was, a good sized lion track, and it looked to be fresh. Immediately, I started encouraging Bo to join in with Pat II, and much to my surprise, he did, and off they went. This was over about as fast as it started. This lion must have crossed the road just ahead of us, because they had it treed within five minutes, and just like that, Bo was a changed dog. I had listened to Bo tree many times by now, but this time there was a different tone in his voice, and when I got to the tree I could see that they were both excited beyond belief. It was easy to see that Bo loved this. Then ten days later these two caught another lion. From that moment on, Bo was a changed dog, and my world of hound hunting was changing right along with him.

1964

Pat II along with his first lion in California. Pat-II had been on others before I got him, so he at least knew what they were, but this was Bo's first.

These two caught it together at McFarland Creek in the Greenhorn Mountains.

This was all it took; then everything changed.

"I started catching lions."

Chapter 3

RUBE CREEK

Now that I had both Bo, and Pat, I started directing most of my attention to hunting in the Greenhorn Mountains. With every opportunity that I had, I would take time off from my job in construction and head for the mountains to hunt. This was not simply for a weekend hunt; instead, it was as close to fulltime as one can get, and still hold down a job. Then, in early November I would leave work, and continue hunting fulltime until April. I did this without stopping, and I went wherever I could in Ventura, Santa Barbara, Kern, or Tulare counties. My favorite was the Greenhorn Mountains of Kern and Tulare counties. During the years of 1964 and 1965, I kept a written log of exactly where, when, and what happened, good or bad. I wanted to know and remember everything that happened. Eventually I tired of the paperwork, so after that I had to rely on memory, and any photographs to keep track of what I had done. I felt that it was more important to know what I was going to do tomorrow, than it was to spend time writing down what I had done the day before.

During that period, I really liked to hunt for bobcats. Everything else came in second and so on down the line. If I caught a lion, well, that was considered a bonus. Almost all of this hunting was on bare ground where I would let the dogs hunt ahead of me and it was up to them to find the track on their own. Because of this, they needed to be broken from running anything that I didn't want them chasing after, such as deer, coyotes, and the like. In the beginning, Bo wanted nothing to do with trailing lions as I stated earlier. Since I partnered Pat II, (who we will refer to as "Pat") up with Bo they were a team. Lions were now becoming paramount in their tracking.

These two dogs were doing very well together, and catching something almost every time their feet hit the ground. Between November second and the end of the year, these two dogs had racked up a couple of lions, and over thirty small game animals such as bobcats and foxes while hunting in the higher regions of the Southern Sierras. Then on December 30, I was hunting on the Piute Mountain in Kern County, and didn't find anything there, so on December 31, I went to Pine Flat and started hunting the Johnsondale Road that travels between Pine Flat and Johnsondale. The area was always a better than average place to hunt for the kind of animals that I was looking for, and most of the terrain was usually easy to get around in, so that worked well with what I was doing.

As soon as I got there it started off with a bang. Green grass and clear skies, I caught a bobcat right off on the thirty-first, and then on the first of January, I caught another one. By mid-morning, it started to snow. Temperatures dropped into the single digits and it continued to snow until about 1 a.m. on the morning of January second, 1965. With fresh snow and clear skies, I couldn't ask for anything better. I decided to wait until daylight and then see if I could find any lion tracks. I had set up my camp on the Johnsondale Road where it crossed Deer Creek, and the snow at that elevation, (3800 feet,) was only about two inches deep.

I left camp at daybreak to look for tracks in the snow and the further I traveled up the road the deeper the snow got. After I had gone about six miles, with no sign of anything except for a couple of deer tracks, I found myself at about 5500 feet in elevation and between Dead Mule Saddle and Cold Springs Saddle. I could see that the snow was getting deep enough that I wasn't going to be able to go much further. Then, there they were: fresh lion tracks crossing the road, coming from the east and heading down into Cold Springs Creek.

It was now around 8 a.m., this is good, and I couldn't ask for anything better. The tracks were fresh enough that it couldn't have been more than six hours since the lion had been there, and it looked like this one was going to be easy. I strapped on my gun, closed up my truck, and showed Bo and Pat the tracks. They both stuck their noses into a track, and off they went covering ground as fast as they could go, their heads straight into the air as if they were following the trail just by sight. I fell in right behind them, and within ten minutes, they were so far ahead of me that they were completely out of hearing range. All I could do now was to start following their tracks. Because of the deep snow, it was easy to see where they had gone, however, because of the steep terrain and deep snow the going wasn't all that fast; that's okay, they are after a lion, and I'll find them.

The lion had gone down Cold Springs Creek for about two miles paralleling the road that I had just come up, then crossed over to another creek called Merry Creek. From here it went down Merry Creek for about two miles and then turned, heading west for about another mile. From there I followed their tracks over a mountain saddle that went between Tyler Peak and another small mountain peak just to the north of it and into some private land, where it started to skirt the east side of Rube Creek. It was there that the snow was starting to disappear, making it difficult in some places to follow the dogs. For the first time since starting out, I had to start to second-guess the direction I needed to take.

I found what appeared to be an old trail that was heading north and on the east side of Rube Creek, so I got onto it and started walking towards the north. It looked like this might be a likely place that the lion would go, so I starting heading that way. After about a half-mile or so, I got lucky: there they were, one lion track with both dogs right alongside it. The lion was now heading to the north and after going another couple miles, they crossed Cold Springs Creek, only this time they were a couple of miles down creek from where they crossed it earlier. This lion was now heading almost straight uphill and back into the higher elevations of the National Forest. From there it crossed over another small ridge, and dropped right into the bottom of Rube Creek,

I had never been in Rube Creek before, but I had heard that it was full of steep rock cliffs covered with heavy oak, Manzanita, and chaparral brush. When you add all this together, it can make it extremely hard for both dogs and man to get through any of it, and this is what I was now looking at. At this point, it made no difference how rough it was, I could see that the dogs were still after it, and as long as I could see their tracks along with the lion's, I would not quit. So far, I had been pushing myself as hard as I could for hours, covered many miles over steep terrain and without the snow, it was easy to see that I would have lost them. Only, I hadn't lost them—I just couldn't hear them. They had gone far enough by now that I expected to find them every time I crossed over another ridge or dropped into another drainage, but that wasn't happening. I had no choice except to keep on going.

Now, I could see that they were heading straight up the bottom of Rube Creek and after they went about a quarter mile they pulled out of the bottom and started climbing up the west side of the creek, and onto a ridge that came off of a mountain peak known as Buck Slide. This lion was covering some rugged ground and had gone right through several areas that had quite a few deer in them and I couldn't help but wonder what it was up to. It obviously wasn't looking for something to eat, evidenced by the number of fresh deer signs that it had passed up, so my best guess was that it was simply traveling, maybe looking for another lion. I had no idea of where or how far ahead of me they were, and it was easy to see that the further they went the rougher it got.

By now it was getting late in the day, and I still had not heard either Bo or Pat since I first turned them loose that morning. I had travelled over ten air miles, and after going about another mile up the west side of Rube Creek I finally started to hear something that sounded like it might be them. Whatever it was that I had heard, it was so far away that at first it was only very faint sounds that would come and go, and I had to pause and listen to make sure of what I was hearing. These two dogs sounded completely different when trailing and treeing. Pat had a steady chop when trailing and he still chopped when treeing, just a little faster, which made it a little difficult to determine the difference with him, but Bo was easy. When trailing he was all bawl mouth and when he treed he let loose with a deep, heavy short bark, and that is what I thought I had heard. I kept climbing the ridge and after going an additional couple of hundred yards, I heard them again. It sounded like they were still quite a distance from where I was at, but it was them, no doubt about it. As I kept pushing forward, the sounds started to become more and more clear to me: they were treed, and they were barking so hard it sounded like they were trying to blow the top right off the tree! I still had a long hard climb to go, but it was them; they got it, and they were telling the world about it.

They were about another mile ahead of me and just a little below Buck Slide, close to 6,000 feet in elevation, and close to crossing over the main backbone ridge that runs between Parker Peak and North Cold Springs Peak, with the Tule Indian Reservation on the opposite side. By the time I got to them, the sun was starting to drop out of sight behind the ridges of the Coastal Mountain Range. I had no idea how long they had been under that tree, but I did know I had not seen them for about eight hours and when I got there the only one that was not happy to see me was the lion. It was an average-sized female of about a hundred pounds and she was nervous to say the least; as soon as I got there she looked like she was ready to jump out and I couldn't let that happen. She was about halfway up a mostly dead pine tree that was only about thirty feet tall. It was growing out of an extremely steep and rocky ridge that had barely enough room for just one dog to stand on it at a time, let alone both dogs and myself. The sides of this ridge were of loose rocks that dropped straight off on each side and there wasn't another tree within fifty feet in any direction.

With all I'd gone through to find the three of them, I couldn't let it jump out, so I needed to act quick. There was just enough daylight left to shoot it, skin it out, and get my bearing on how to get back to my truck. I put both Bo and Pat on their leashes and held them with my left hand as I aimed my Ruger .22 mag. with my right, it took just one shot, and it was over. Well, halfway over. I still needed to skin the lion out and return to my truck, which was a long way off.

I was soaking wet to the bone because of the melting snow that had soaked into my clothing and boots, I had no flashlight and a freshly skinned lion hide draped over my shoulders. I kept Bo and Pat snapped together with a pair of couplers and we started heading back. The daytime temperatures did get to a little above freezing in the sunlit areas, but when it turned dark, the temperatures started to drop into the single digits again. That was okay, there was nothing I could do about that anyway; the important thing was we were all back together again and heading out of there as fast as we could. But we had a long way to go, especially in the dark.

It was about 5 p.m. when we started back. At first it was all downhill, in fact it was about a 3,500 foot drop in elevation just to get back to where I had crossed Rube Creek a few hours earlier. I knew that the only safe way to do this was to backtrack myself as best as I could, so I stayed on the same ridge that I had climbed up to where the dogs had treed. Then I got myself back to where I pulled out of Rube Creek, went down Rube Creek about a half mile, then headed east, to find Cold Springs Creek. The sun had completely set by the time I walked into the bottom of Rube Creek and now I needed to find my way back in the dark as we headed due east to Cold Springs Creek. Fortunately, my eyes were adjusting to the darkness, and the sky was clear enough that the brightness of the stars actually did give some light, especially when we were in the snow. I felt that under the present conditions, I was making pretty good time as we pulled out of Rube

Creek and were heading due east. From there, I went straight east to Cold Springs Creek. I was able to cut off about three miles by not going around the small mountain that I had gone around earlier, and skipping Merry Creek altogether.

Still, I needed to be very careful. Once we got back into tall timber, the darker it got, the harder it was, and now it was only one step at a time, and the last thing I needed was to get turned around. It was almost 8 p.m. when I had reached Cold Springs Creek. So far so good, then I found my own foot tracks in the snow where I had come down earlier that day, so I knew it was all uphill and only about two miles back to the truck. We climbed up this canyon for about an hour or so when I needed to take a break. I'd been going for about thirteen hours without stopping except to kill and skin the lion, and the small bowl of oatmeal that I had around 6:00 a.m. earlier that morning had worn off. By then I had travelled about fifteen air miles in steep terrain, breaking my way through knee-deep snow in some places, or pushing against snow-covered heavy brush in others. At the start, I had dropped down about 2,000 feet in elevation from where the lion first crossed the road, then climbed up another 3,500 feet to the dogs and lion, then turned around and dropped back down that same 3,500 feet, and all I had left was about a five miles hike in total darkness, and climb another 2,000 foot climb back to my truck. At that point it didn't matter: we had done it! I loved it—this was lion hunting at its best.

For the first time since heading back, I needed to take a breather. I found an open spot in a clearing where the snow was almost all gone; the ground was definitely frozen, but I didn't care. I laid the lion hide on the ground with the hair up, wrapped myself with it as best I could, pulled Bo and Pat up next to me, and fell asleep. At somewhere around 10 PM, I was awakened by the sound of Pat chewing on the lion hide. I had been wet and somewhat cold all day long, and as soon as the sun went down my soaking wet clothes had started to freeze. As I lie there on the hide, the cold I had been feeling before didn't feel the same; my feet were almost burning from it. The temperature must have been in the single digits, and only getting colder as the night went on. By now, I knew I was in trouble, or at least my feet were. I needed to start moving again, and I knew that it wouldn't be light again for a long time, but if I was going to avoid hypothermia, and frost bite, I had to get moving.

I wasn't too sure of my exact location, and thought that I may have got onto a wrong ridge or even was in the wrong canyon, but I needed to get moving. I felt that if I wasn't back to my truck by the time the sun came up, I would be able to warm up by standing in the sunlight. I looked to the east and I could see the silhouette of the mountain ridges against the night sky. So, I picked out the tallest one and said to myself, that's the one I will climb first. I grabbed up the lion hide, threw it over my shoulders, told Pat and Bo to come with me and we started climbing, and what a surprise I had waiting for me. We had gone maybe three hundred feet when I found myself standing in the road with my truck less than a quarter a mile away.

Needless to say, it took me no time to get there. When I first bought this truck, I had built myself an enclosed camper where I could sleep on a bed just over the dog boxes below. The first thing I did was put Bo and Pat into the camper in their dog boxes under my bed. Then I started the motor to get the cab warmed up and fired up the Coleman stove in the camper to get some heat in there. I had an unopened one-quart can of cran-apple juice in the food cooler and I drank it so fast that I almost inhaled it. I fed Bo and Pat their usual ration of Purina High Pro dog food. Next, I opened a can of Dinty Moore beef stew and while that was warming on the stove, I took off my boots and found that my socks were covered with ice. Wet and cold is one thing, but when I was resting, I had no idea what was happening inside my boots. That was when I got my first lesson in frostbite, a lesson that would stay with me for the rest of my life.

In the years that followed, I caught lions that were easily caught, short races that would only last 30 minutes from start to finish, and I called them pop ups. Most of those hunts were forgotten about in no time at all.

But this one is the kind that makes memories. One man, one lion, two dogs, and mile after mile of trailing, then treed. I couldn't get enough of it.

Chapter 4

DEAD MULE SADDLE

After returning to Ventura, I needed to take my new 1965 Chevrolet 4 X 4 ½ ton pickup truck back into the dealer in Ojai, California for the new vehicle inspection before it ran past the 3,000 miles allowed by the manufacturer. This got me to visiting with the salesman who sold me the truck. He was quite the character. I do remember his name, but to avoid him any embarrassments, I will call him C.J. C.J. said he hunted all the time for ducks and geese, which his office walls were covered with stuffed birds of all kinds, and he wanted to go hunting with me. He went on to tell me that he had never hunted with hounds before and he just wanted to see what this hound hunting was all about. I invited him along and I told him that if he really wanted to go, he would need to drive his own vehicle to California Hot Springs, where I would meet him in just a few days. At first, I didn't know if he would really show up, but on January eighth at just before dark, he was there. He brought everything he needed for camping, gun and all.

I did a lot of night hunting when looking for bobcats so at about 9 PM, we headed out on the road from California Hot Springs to Johnsondale and by 11 PM, Bo and Pat treed a bobcat. It was an easy catch where the dogs caught it within an hour from the time they started trailing it. C.J. shot it and from there we decided to get some rest and start again at sun up.

The weather had warmed up considerably over the past week and there was no snow anywhere below 5,500 feet. All of the hunting was to be done on bare ground with the dogs turned loose to find the tracks all on their own.

We were camping at my usual site, alongside Johnsondale Road, where Deer Creek crossed underneath it. When we caught the bobcat we were only a mile from camp, so when we started again in the morning I thought it would be best to travel a little further up the road. I let the two dogs out about a mile before we got to Merry Camp and started road hunting them from there. When they got about a mile past Dead Mule Saddle they found the tracks of a lion that had come out of Alder Creek, which was just to the east of us, and trailed it down into Cold Springs Creek. Unlike the one that I caught only the week before, this one went straight across the canyon and onto the other side. From there, it climbed up the opposite side of the creek, and once it got onto the main backbone of that ridge, it turned north toward Hatchet Peak. This track was fresh and easy for the dogs to trail and didn't take long for them to catch up with it. When they treed it, they were less than a hundred yards from the top of the Hatchet Peak. It was perfect! They had trailed it only about two miles before catching it and we were able to listen to them go all the way from start to tree by staying in the road and moving in the same direction that they were going.

We parked the truck just below Cold Springs Saddle, crossed Cold Springs Creek, and had an easy hike to where the dogs were treed. My friend was doing okay keeping up with me until we started a steep climb out of the creek. From there on he seemed to be slowing down, and I kept moving at my normal pace, and continued doing that until I got to the tree. The lion was in a small pine that had grown out of a bunch of rocks on a very steep hillside. There were only few places where we could hike up this ridge and get to the tree, and all of that was a straight up climb from below. Once I arrived at the tree I was able to walk around it okay, but there was barely enough room for me, the two dogs, and hopefully the other guy. I kept calling for him to hurry up because the lion was looking all around and making me think it was wanting to jump out. I wasn't sure if that happened that C.J. could make the climb to another tree.

After about five minutes, I could see C.J. slowly coming from below, following in the same path I had walked, but he didn't seem like he really wanted to come up to us. He kept stopping to ask me questions. Then he would stand and wait for an answer before going any further. I had to keep telling him over and over to get a move on, but he seemed to be walking in slow motion. He started to climb again and just as he got within sixty to seventy feet of where we were, he looked up and saw that the lion, and noticed that it was looking right at him. This scared him so bad that when the lion shifted just to get more comfortable, he froze again and started yelling at me, and wanting to know, "Why is it looking at me?" Over and over again he kept yelling this. I had to wait for him to stop yelling before I could call back and tell him that the lion wanted to jump out of this tree and that he was standing on the only path that the lion could use to do this! That did it; he immediately started yelling, "Stop!" as loud as he could.

At the same time he turned around and started running down the hill as fast as he could go, stumbling, yelling to stop and almost falling down with every step, all the way. I had never seen anything like it! All I could do was holler at him to stop. I'm totally stunned at what was happening. Here this guy makes an about face, and starts running down the hillside and at the same time the lion jumps out, landing about 40 feet above the spot where he started running from, then it passes by him within a fraction of a second, and only about a foot away from him. Then here comes Bo and Pat hot after the lion. C.J. was running hysterically down the canyon, waving both of his arms, and yelling all the way until the lion with the dogs passed him. All the while, he was sounding as though the Devil himself was hot on his heels and about to catch him. The dogs quickly faded out of hearing as they literally flew down the canyon chasing the lion.

I hurried as fast as I could to catch up with him and try to settle him down. At first he was so shook up that I had him sit down on a rock and try to catch his breath. Besides being embarrassed, he was very apologetic, but in his mind he was positive that this lion was out to get him. After giving him a few minutes to pull himself together, I told him that we needed to get a move on and find where the dogs and lion had gone. Then I told him that I was sure that they had caught the lion again, so let's go. With that, he got up and we started hiking back out of the canyon and back to my truck. From there we drove back down the road, and by the time we got close to Merry Camp we could hear the dogs treeing in the bottom of the canyon. From there, we left the truck and headed towards the dogs that were less than a half-mile away. This time, they were in an area that was easy to get around in, and the lion was treed in a black oak tree. By the time we got to this second tree he had somewhat calmed down enough to where he could actually get to within shooting distance, which was still quite a long shot. Instead of standing at the base of the tree and shooting almost straight up, he stood about two hundred feet away from the tree, which gave him an almost level shot at the lion. Because he was still a little nervous, I was concerned that he would either run out of bullets shooting at it or even worse, just wound it. He was shaking and very nervous, therefore, I strongly suggested that he bench-rest his rifle against a tree to shoot while I waited at the bottom of the tree, with my gun ready, just in case. Then after fifteen minutes of catching his breath, he calmly fired, and got it with one shot.

We then packed the lion down the canyon to Merry Camp, then out onto the road. I left him with it and walked back up the road to get the truck. From there, C.J. went back to Ojai with a fresh lion and bobcat hide, and a fistful of photos to put on his office wall.

Two weeks later I needed to go back to the Chevrolet dealership in Ojai and when I pulled in to the service area, the service manager and his assistant approached me. The two of them started off telling me about the hunt that their car salesman C.J. had gone to the Sierra's. They knew that I hunted for lions and I would probably like to talk with him. As we were standing just outside C.J.'s office they started telling me all about C.J.'s hunt in the Sierra's. According to C.J., he found a lion track and was in the process of following it when he heard something behind him; then as he was turning around he saw the lion as it was flying in the air towards him and just as it was about to land on him, he shot and killed it. It sounded to me that they knew something was fishy with C.J.'s story, so they made sure that he got to hear them talking outside. These two lead the way into his office and as I followed close behind them, the manager said, hey C.J., there's a guy here that wants to talk with you. Everyone was laughing by that time including C.J. who said, "Ah, you caught me". They did just that, C.J. was actually quite the character and I never did tell any of them what actually happened, but they knew C.J. He was fun to be around, however, I don't think I would buy a used car from him.

C.J's Mountain Lion

January 9, 1966
Myself with Bo and Pat
On the Johnsondale Rd.
Where it crosses Tyler Creek

Chapter 5

SAYLOR

I CONTINUED TO HUNT WITH J.D. Reynolds as much as possible, and in time, he told me that Bo was raised by a man named Elbert Vaughn. Elbert was a very well-known breeder of Bluetick Hounds in Paragould, Arkansas and personal friend of J. D.'s, who also grew up there. Elbert had developed a particular strain of dogs that by all accounts were considered outstanding in ability and looks and I thought that helped to explain a lot about Bo, who was actually Redtick in color. Until the 1950's the only difference in Redtick and Bluetick was their color. Before that time they were both English Coon Hounds. Many of Elbert's Blueticks became the foundation stock for some of the best hunting dogs known for small and big game hunting. While visiting and hunting with J.D., he went on to tell me that in his opinion, Bo was nothing special as compared to some of the other dogs he had seen come from Elbert, whom he suggested I contact if I was interested in starting with young dogs. That sounded good to me, so it looked like it was time for me to take a trip to Arkansas.

I contacted Elbert and made arrangements for a visit. It was early May of 1965 when I arrived at his farm, with Bo and Pat. I was eager to see what he had, hoping to learn as much as possible from the visit and maybe pick up another dog from him. I stayed with him and his wife Sara until the end of July. It was easy to see that they both knew their dogs very well and Elbert soon took a liking to me. He offered me a job where I would stay there to hunt his dogs for him and enter them in field trials and shows. Elbert worked in a shoe factory fulltime, so the time he could dedicate to hunting was somewhat limited. The offer was quite flattering, but wasn't what I had in mind for my future, and I really didn't care for that part of the country. So, I declined the offer, but continued with my visit and we hunted at least three nights a week. I also became very familiar with his dogs, and met several other well-known hunters who lived around that part of the country. In a short time, it was very easy to see that all his dogs were as J.D. said: exceptionally good. After almost three months with Elbert, I was ready to head back west and into the higher mountains of California. But before leaving, I was still hoping to get a young dog from him.

When I arrived, he had four pairs of pups running around his farm, all about four to five months old. They were all from different crosses and each pair had one male and one female. There was plenty of room for these young dogs to run around and still stay out of trouble on his farm. This gave each of them a good opportunity to learn to trail and run by chasing rabbits. Also, by allowing this they would develop the spirit of chasing something, and at the same time, Elbert could see what they were like and choose which ones he would keep and which he would sell, when it came time. This gave me the opportunity to rate them as well. In fact, I saw more of them than Elbert did while I was staying on and helping on the farm, since he worked five days a week.

These little guys all looked very good to me, and I really hoped to get one of them. I don't think Elbert was quite ready to part with any just yet, and like dealing with Willis, I knew this could get hard. What was I to do? I couldn't hang around for another four to six months waiting for him to decide, and I didn't want to leave empty-handed, either. So one day, right up front I said, "Elbert, you have eight pups here, and I want to buy one of them. How about you pick the one you don't want and sell it to me?"

His answer was simple: "I don't know yet, I think I like them all." Well, that's not what I was wanting or expecting to hear from him. Then at the dinner table that night he up and asked his wife, Sara, if she would be willing to sell me the male pup out of their female called Lula II. I couldn't believe what Elbert had just said. I had watched all of these pups chasing rabbits around his farm for almost three months, and although he wasn't the best looking in the bunch, he was definitely the fastest, and he would have been my first choice. Sara kind of acted like she didn't want to let any of them go just yet, but eventually put a price out there of two hundred dollars. Now, I don't know if they were trying to discourage me or not with that price, but if that was what they were hoping for it didn't work. I bought him right then and there, and he was known as "Saylor" from that day forward. I stayed for a few more days before heading home. I was so grateful for the time I had spent with Elbert and Sara on the farm. Because of their friendship, I had really made headway in creating a good bunch of dogs for my future hunting.

I was happy now, returned to working in the housing tracts of Thousand Oaks for a couple of months until the rainy season started. Then, I went to my boss and asked for more time off. He was a good guy, liked me quite a bit, and asked how long I would be gone. I told him I would probably be back in five or six months. He didn't know what to say, except he never heard of anything like this before and hoped I would come back, I could have a job working with him anytime I wanted it. But, I never saw him again. I was a framer and that work had already taken a toll on my back. I was having so much trouble with it that I was going to a chiropractor about once a week just to be able to stand up straight. I had also gone to an orthopedic surgeon who said that I needed to have my lower back fused in a few places. This guy went on to tell me that he was surprised that I could even walk, and the more that he explained to me what this surgery was about, the closer I got to the door. As I left his office, he told me that within twelve months I would be crawling back to him, begging for the operation. I couldn't get out of there fast enough. I could still work, just not as a framer, and I had no problems hunting, so whenever I needed straightening out, it was off to the chiropractor and then back to the woods.

I hunted all of that winter, mostly by myself with my three dogs. Saylor was old enough to put in with Bo and Pat by the end of October and he came on stronger than I ever expected. By spring I was faced with a decision of what to do with Pat. I liked him; in fact, I liked him a lot. He was no trouble at all, didn't run deer and coyotes or anything, other than the game animals that I wanted to hunt. But he was a little slower on a fast moving track than Bo, plus he couldn't come close to running with Saylor, which was the main problem. Because of this, I decided it would be best to let him go to someone where he would be of help, so that's what I did. Now, I was back to just two dogs again and looking for another, hopefully a Bluetick from the Vaughn strain. I couldn't believe that I was now parting with a dog that was actually good, but not good enough, but that's just what I did.

As I've mentioned, I had started making a ledger of my hunting experiences when I first got Bo. I continued to write down everything that happened, whether we caught anything or not, and after a total of fifty-seven days of Bo, Pat and Saylor hunting together, they treed a total of eighty-five game animals. I was obviously impressed beyond belief with this kind of success. In addition to that, they had caught one bear and four lions, which I was very happy with, since neither one of them had any experience with either of those animals before I got them. The rest were bobcats, foxes, and a few raccoons.

Spring was on the way now and I was in the market again for Pat's replacement. Elbert was booked up on pups for the next year, so that ruled out getting anything from him. I needed to look elsewhere. I had met a guy about two years older than me while at Elbert's who was from Mississippi. He had a Bluetick that was around four-years-old and came from an outstanding cross of Elbert's dogs. He seemed to be very honest, which I was learning was not one of the more common characteristics in hound hunters, so we hit it off. He built homes there and offered me a job as a carpenter if I was interested, which I wasn't, at the time. I was, however, interested in making a trip to where he lived to just see what swamp hunting was like, since this was where my interest first started, when I was working at GM on the assembly line.

So in the spring 1966, I went to the heart of Dixie. I stayed with Bob Denley and his family at their home, in Grenada, Mississippi, and they were wonderful people. But what an experience it was: hot, swampy marshland full of huge mosquitoes, timber rattlers and raccoons. Every time we went hunting we would tree at least one raccoon, and at the same time, we were chasing the dogs, they were chasing the raccoons, and we were being chased by millions of mosquitoes. That place was different than anyplace I had been to before. I hunted with several good hounds while there, worked for Bob on a couple of his housing projects after all, but I really wasn't cut out for that place. In about mid-July I loaded up Bo and Saylor and we headed back to California and the Greenhorn Mountains of the Southern Sierra's, only this time, I was moving there. I had no idea of what I was going to do for a living, or if I could even make a living there. But I thought I'd figure all that out later.

At first, I simply lived in the back of my truck, which was now a one year old Chevrolet 4 x 4 ½ ton, that I bought new the year before. As I stated, I had built a camper shell with dog boxes and a sleeping area above for me. I stayed living that way for several months, living from one campsite to another. After moving to Glennville I got a job cutting firewood for a guy who resold it out of his yard in Glennville. He provided me with a two-ton truck and a place where I could go and cut the trees. I had to provide my own saw, tools, gas and anything else I needed. The trees to cut were all oak, and about a twenty-five minute drive from his yard. All I had to do was fell the trees, cut to length, hand split, load, deliver, then unload, make a tight stack of wood in his yard, and he would pay me eighteen dollars for each cord. It wasn't much for this kind of work, but to me it was worth the sacrifice.

I continued living in the back of my truck with Bo and Saylor for about three months. In the meantime, I did my shopping in either Lake Isabella or Glennville. At that time, Glennville had a full service gas station, grocery store, one restaurant, one café, laundromat, and hardware store. In the surrounding area there were several resorts. I preferred the lifestyle, and weather conditions of Glennville over Isabella, so that's where I wanted to live. I didn't really know anyone there, but that didn't matter because all I wanted to do was hunt with my dogs and there was enough territory right there for me to do it in the Sequoia National Forest which was over one million acres and most of it was prime bobcat and lion country.

I could still go hunting in the Los Padres National Forest in Ventura, Santa Barbara, and San Louis Obispo counties. It had lions, no doubt about it, but it wasn't the easiest place to catch them and wasn't my favorite place.

I knew that the Federal Government was growing sensitive to some of their trappers using hounds in this area. Then while I was hunting in the mountains around Cuyama Valley, I ran into my friend Dick Muldoon. Dick was a Government trapper who was sent there to thin out the coyotes in that area. Since I was planning to hunt in the same area as he was trapping in, he invited me to stay at his campsite. I saw no harm in that, so I took him up on the offer. The next day we caught a bobcat and also found fresh tracks of a lion. Then on the next day we caught the lion. Then when Dick's supervisor found out Dick came with me, he fired him. I talked to Dick on the phone right before they let him go, and he said it was basically being done to accommodate a local rancher there who didn't care for him. This was hard for me to understand when Dick was also trapping bobcats and coyotes in the same area, and this usually benefitted the ranchers. Dick was an exceptionally good trapper and I never could understand why this happened. But there was nothing I could do about it. I considered this, my formal introduction to one of the more unpleasant ways the Government sometimes operate.

1967

Saylor and me at Dick Muldoon's camp with a bobcat and a female lion that we caught in the low canyons of the Los Padres National Forest just South of New Cuyama

Chapter 6

GLENNVILLE

By 1966, I had spent almost six years trying to stay out of the crowds and cities and simply do my hunting. There wasn't anything that I enjoyed as much as hunting, and if I could make a career by hunting with my dogs, I was going to do it. I lived with these dogs, to the point that I was pretty sure they knew what I was thinking most of the time, and I felt the same about them. It was like we were a family, or at least the very best of friends. I had been living in the camper on my truck, in the Greenhorn Mountains, for about three months, and didn't want to leave this area. I just wanted someplace with a little more room for my dogs and myself.

So I started asking around to see if I could find a place for rent. I can't remember just who it was, but somebody told me they thought Max App had a place on his ranch that he might rent out. He lived a little further up the road past Glennville. I knew right where it was and just hadn't known who owned it up to that point. He had a nice big house on the north side of the road and only about a mile from town. I didn't call first, just drove in to see if this was true. He said it was and that it would be forty-five dollars a month, including electricity and water. Max told me that his boy, John, would take me there, and if I liked it I could move in anytime. Just no hunting of any kind was allowed on his property. That was okay with me. I just needed a place for me and my dogs before the winter set in.

It wasn't exactly what I expected for the price, but I said I'd take it. I wasn't sure who lived in it before me, or how long it had been since they had been there, but it was pretty rough. Someone started out with an old travel trailer that was about sixteen feet long by eight feet wide, and then added a wooden lean-to of about the same size on one side. Most of the windows were broken in the trailer, and the lean-to had window screening all around that started at about four feet above the floor and went to the ceiling. To keep the cold and wind out, all these openings were covered with clear plastic visqueen, most of which were full of holes. It had an army-type cot in the trailer part, as well as in the lean-to. For heat it had a nice, century-old, wood-burning cook stove, and there were iron pipe coils that ran through the firebox to heat the water for the sink and bathroom shower, which was enclosed by tin walls and a curtain for a door.

There was a piece of six inch well casing about five feet tall that served as the hot water storage. It had a half inch iron pipe coming off this six inch pipe that went into the wood cook stove firebox, where the fire heated it and from there it went back into the well-casing until needed. There was also a hot water relief valve on top of the casing that would blow off the excess water if it got too hot, and the pressure built up too high. When that happened it was so loud and banged so hard that the entire trailer would actually shake. This combined with the fact that the firebox was so small it needed to be filled about every forty-five minutes, which made it so inconvenient that there was no way it could be used for nighttime heat.

Regardless, the water-heating design was clever, and the instructions were very simple: first, the wood had to be split small enough to fit into the firebox, which was smaller than most because of the iron pipes that were used to heat the water, and once the fire was kept going for about an hour, you had about six gallons of hot water. The stove was also the only form of heat Max allowed. With the winter night temperatures dropping into the lower teens or even to single digits, it could get cold in there. It did have electricity, so I invested in two electric blankets, one for myself, and the other for anyone who stayed with me. I built Bo and Saylor each a dog house of their own and put plenty of straw bedding in for them. So we were home.

It didn't take long before I started to meet some of the Glennville natives. Most were very friendly and even welcomed me to the community. The first of the old-time ranchers that I met was Jack Lavers. His family was part of the very first to settle there over a hundred years earlier. He was very friendly towards me, and in time I learned that this guy was a true gentleman. As word spread that I had moved to the area, it didn't take long before I was introduced to most of the permanent residents who lived close by. Eventually, I was offered the opportunity to rent a house right in the middle of Glennville, a town with a population of about three hundred at the time, and that was only if you counted everyone within fifteen miles. Otherwise the sign entering town read something like, Population 35.

Moving from that trailer to town didn't take much thought, especially with the savings of ten dollars a month. It was now spring of 1966, and the house was no doubt much older than the trailer I was moving out of, but it was a house. It had a kitchen, bathroom, two bedrooms, living room and fireplace. It also had a one-car garage, with a dirt floor and plenty of space for my dogs, and even room for a horse, if I wanted one.

Eventually, I was told by an old-time rancher that next to an old adobe building that was an historical monument, it was the oldest house in Glennville, and it sure looked like it just might have been. He said that it was there when he was a kid and that it was already very old then, so it had to have been built sometime in the late 1800s. I didn't mind. I took it and was happy to get it. My move was quick and easy since all I owned was my truck, two electric blankets and two hound dogs and their wooden houses.

The type of construction used to build this house was called the California Box. That meant rough lumber was used throughout. It had one two-by-four top and bottom plate, a two-by-four stud at each corner, the only other two-by-fours wrapped around the window and door openings, then one-by-twelve cedar boards placed vertically to the outside and nailed, with square nails to the plates. These served as both the siding and wall studs all at the same time. The outside had one-by-three battens nailed at the seams, and then they cut holes through the siding to place the windows and doors in, and any nails that went through the siding that were visible on the inside were simply bent over. The inside walls were wallpapered and that was the only thing that kept the wind from blowing through the house; there was no insulation anywhere.

The fireplace had no smoke chamber or damper, so when it rained hard enough (and many times it did), the fire was extinguished by the water coming straight down the chimney. After bringing this problem up to my landlord, who also ran the grocery store and lived right in front of this house, he installed a gas heater for me and had a butane bottle put in. I just had to pay for the gas. It also had a small garage that came with it, and shortly after moving in I asked my landlord if it would be okay with him if I could keep an occasional live lion in it, which he had no problem with. Out of curiosity he asked me how I was able to catch them alive, and I told him it was simple. I simply pulled them out of the tree with a rope and then stuffed them into a 55 gallon barrel. He said, You do what! I got to see that.

All and all, it was a good move. My rent was now only thirty-five dollars per month, which saved me enough to have a telephone installed, and this was important since I was going to start advertising as a hunting guide in the hunting magazines. It also put me right in town and by being there I was able to meet people much faster and easier, which of course was another big step for me.

In the beginning, the only thing I ever dreamed of was hunting with hounds, and now I was actually doing it as a professional. I was twenty five years old, had two very good dogs, a 4X4 half ton pickup truck that was less than two years old, lived in an area where I didn't need to go far to hunt, and I was poor as a church mouse. I continued cutting oak firewood for my friend at the rate of eighteen dollars per cord, delivered and stacked, and occasionally I would be asked to do it for some of the cabin owners at a rate of twenty-five dollars per cord. I would do any carpentry jobs that I could find and I also had about six months of unemployment insurance to help with my expenses.

I started advertising in Outdoor Life Magazine, and a one-month ad cost as much as my rent. The normal fee at that time for a successful lion hunt was $500, and bobcats were fifty bucks. The only catch was that all competing guides were offering no-catch no-pay hunts, which meant that the guide only got paid after a successful hunt. This could be tough. But that's the way it was and if I was going to do this, that's what it paid, or didn't pay. Since I had no printed brochure to hand out I needed to write back in the form of a letter; so now I needed a typewriter. I couldn't afford a new one. So, I picked up an old used Royal at a pawn shop, got some stationery printed up in Bakersfield to make it look a little more professional, along with matching envelopes, and carbon paper so I could keep copies for myself. There was also a lady who lived in Glennville, who was a graphic artist. I believed she worked for a Bakersfield newspaper. For a very small amount of money she made a poster that I could attach a photo to, which I framed and placed in most of the businesses in the area. I obtained my California Guide License, which was strictly a formality, and I was ready to go. All I needed now was customers.

In the years prior to my arrival, there was only one other person that had lived in this area, as a professional hunter, and that was Howard Bilton, who died in 1961. Howard had worked as one of the few fulltime professional California State lion hunters and received a salary from the state, plus expenses, and he also got the bounty that was paid out for killing them. Unlike Howard, it made no difference how many lions I caught; I was freelance, paid all my own expenses and only got paid when I caught something, and only then if I had a paying customer with me. There were quite a number of other hunters who were hunting with dogs in that area, but they were mostly bobcat and coon hunters and they seemed to hunt on private ranches far more than in the higher elevations of the National Forest.

It didn't take long after moving to Glennville that, I wanted to know more about the lion hunters who came before me, so I wrote to the California Fish & Game Department and asked for the records on a few State and private hunters, Howard included. What a surprise that was! Some of these state hunters really took a lot of lions. Those with the most recorded kills were Jay Bruce, Charley Ledshaw, and Howard Bilton. Most of this all happened long before I was born, and those days were a distant history not too likely to be repeated by anyone. Bruce, Ledshaw, and Bilton, along with others, had all hunted where I was now living, and these facts should have told me that, this place had been hit pretty hard. I soon came to understand that there wasn't nearly as many lions for me to hunt as when these earlier men hunted here. I couldn't come close to taking what they could back then. So, Glennville eventually became my base of operations, and in time I would need to branch out to other areas, including other states, if I was going to make a living as a professional hunter.

In no time at all, local parents started asking if their teenage boys could go with me, and I gladly accepted. As usual, I informed the parents that I didn't always come home on the same day that I left. Much to my surprise, the parents trusted me enough to take the boys regardless of how long we were gone. This made me feel really good to know that they trusted me that way, and I could only wish that kind of opportunity had been available to me when I was their age.

One such boy was a fifteen year old who lived in Glennville, and was the son of Jim Stephenson, a fireman who was stationed at the firehouse there. The Stephenson's had a dairy cow where I had been buying raw milk from the family for some time. I knew them fairly well and Roy was fifteen years old and their oldest. He was a good kid and game for anything. He was already doing odd jobs, milked the cow every day, loved to participate in the annual rodeo, and now he was wanting to go lion hunting.

Our first time out together was in late November, we started at sunup and hunted all day, and then just about sunset when we finally found where a lion had crossed the Basket Pass Road, right at the summit. The track was no doubt made the night before, so this lion was somewhere between twelve to twenty-four hours or so ahead of us. It looked to be a female of average size and I thought it might be one that I had seen tracks of several times before in the Sandy Creek area. I had never treed her before, but the size and shape of her front feet looked very familiar to me. I talked over our situation with Roy, told him that it could be easy or it could be tough, depending on where the lion was. We had seen quite a few fresh deer tracks in the area and if she had been able to kill one, then she could be close by. On the other hand, she could be just traveling, and if that was the case, we could be in for a long haul, especially with her having come through so long ago. Roy said that he didn't care where it had gone or what we had to go through to catch it, he wanted to see a lion up a tree.

First thing we did was to try Bo and Saylor on the track to see if they could pick up any scent. At first, they had a little trouble smelling it, but then after a few minutes they started moving on their own and off they went at a fairly good clip. We had only one flashlight between the two of us, grabbed it up, and off we went into the tall timber, deep canyons, and fading sunset. It was about 5 p.m. when they started heading south around the east side of Basket Peak at around 6,000 feet in elevation, then it turned to the west towards Windmill Tree Peak. By the time they got half way around Windmill Tree Peak, the sun had disappeared.

We were in an area where neither of us had been before, but that didn't make any difference. All we had to do was follow the dogs and try to keep track of things, so we didn't get turned around when it came time to go back. With the trail being so old to begin with, the dogs were not moving very fast, but they were making headway and there was no way we could have stopped them even if we wanted to. There were no roads in this area, so we couldn't start out following in the truck, and we're going to do it all on foot. This went on for several hours before we heard the dogs treeing off in the distance and fortunately within range of our hearing.

We arrived at the tree at about 10:30 p.m.. As expected, it was a female, and I was sure she was the one we started out on. We didn't know where we actually were, except for the general idea of the direction we needed to go to get back out. Our first thoughts were to grab up the dogs and let the lion go. We were both hungry and Roy, who was a fast growing boy and consumed all food that was put in front of him, was starved out by then. Not thinking that we would be gone this long, he had brought only one sandwich with him and he had eaten that long before noon. Quite honestly, I wasn't doing much better. We both were complaining about being hungry and figured it would be one or two in the morning before we found our way back to the truck. Since there wasn't anything to eat, I asked Roy if he wanted to try a little mountain lion roasted over an open fire. He wasted no time in giving me his answer: "Shoot it," he said. It was done. It was an easy, clean shot and we skinned it out and cut some meat.

The two of us made our fire, stuck sticks through the meat and started roasting it over the open fire. As hungry as we were, it wasn't as good as we were hoping for. We both came to the same opinion: never again. It was the toughest meat either of us had ever tried to eat. The longer we chewed it, the harder it got. I finished skinning out the lion and we headed back. From then on, whenever Roy would go with me he always had a sack full of sandwiches, plus a bunch of snacks. I was glad that I now had a good hunting partner in Roy. That is, when he wasn't in school, working at the local gas station, running a backhoe for an excavation contractor, or chasing girls.

The next time we hunted together was on December 29, 1966. It was Roy's sixteenth birthday and he wanted to go hunting, so I picked him up at home just before sunrise and we were off to higher country. He had taken an extra large loaf of Wonderbread (the one with all the polka dots on the wrapper) and had made sandwiches out of the entire loaf, then stuffed them back in the plastic sleeve. He brought along some snacks and something to drink. There was a little snow left from the last storm in the higher elevations above Glennville, so we headed up there to see if we could find any lions. We went up highway 155 to Greenhorn Summit first, then headed south through Shirley Meadows. From there we turned off and headed west on an old logging road that went down to Alder Creek.

So far we hadn't seen any tracks and the snow had been melting off to the point that it wasn't doing us much good. We hadn't gone very far down this road and the snow was all but gone. Because of this, we let Bo and Saylor out to hunt the road ahead of us. From there we passed through the old Boy Scout Camp and continued following the road down the mountain. We had gone about two miles and hadn't seen anything except for a few deer tracks and all of a sudden both of the dogs hit the trail of something that recently crossed the road, and they were off and running. The two of them were wasting no time on this one, and it looked and sounded like it was right in front of them.

At first, Roy and I didn't know what they were after, so we started looking for tracks. As we did this, the sounds of the dogs were fading fast as they headed down Bear Creek. From where we were at, it sounded as though they had started to go around the east side of Red Mountain. We still didn't know what they were after, so all we could do was keep following them in the direction that they went. It was almost impossible to see any tracks because of the thick layer of pine needles that were laying on the ground. Finally, as we got to the bottom of the creek we saw one lion track going up a muddy hillside, and along with it were the three dogs right after it. As we hiked up the hill on the west side of Red Mountain, we could hear the dogs again, but they were a long way from us. We could tell that they were not treed and it looked like they were heading towards Basket Pass area, which was about four air miles away from where we were, and with few to no roads in between.

We needed to make a decision about what we were going to do to find them. The country they had headed into was not the easiest to go through because of the steep terrain and mixture of timber and heavy brush. So, we decided that I would follow the dogs on foot and Roy would go back and get the truck, head back up the logging road that we had just come down, and then head towards the Basket Pass area. Along the way he could stop and listen for the dogs. We had a couple of walkie-talkies to help keep us in touch, but in those days they were very large, heavy, and didn't work very well. But they were better than nothing.

I took off on foot in the direction where I had last heard the dogs. I stayed on the east side of Red Mountain, as best I could, and listening down toward Bear Creek. I had gone about a mile when I dropped down into the canyon, crossed Bear Creek, then pulled up onto a ridge where I was within earshot of Lumreau Creek. About a half mile away, I could hear all three of the dogs treeing. They were right in the bottom of the canyon and not too far from the Old Likely Mill site. This area had a few very old cabins at the mine site, but no one seemed to have used them since the closing of the mine. Then, just as I located the dogs, I heard Roy calling me on the walkie-talkie, telling me that he could also hear them and that he was on his way and we could meet each other on the road that went to the old mine.

From there, I cut across the hills and crossed Lumreau Creek, above where the dogs were treed, then I dropped down onto the road and just as I did I saw Roy. Just then the back driver side wheel dropped into a deep muddy rut in the road and bottomed out on the axle. That was okay, we could fix that later. For now, we had a lion up a tree that was only about one-quarter mile away. The two of us headed for the dogs and as soon as we got to the tree, and saw the lion, I shot it. Then we gathered up the dogs, left the lion where it was, and we headed back to the truck.

So, here we were. We had a truck stuck in a ditch with a flat tire and a dead lion in the bottom of a canyon, and neither one of them were going anywhere unless we did something about it. We had decided to fix the truck first and return for the lion later. Once we got back to the truck and started looking the situation over we found that it was buried to the axle on the left back wheel. All I had for a jack was a small bottle jack that came with the truck. That would have worked fine if it could be placed under the axle, but that was not going to work here. After putting our heads together, we came up with an idea: we took an axe that I had in the truck and found a small cedar about eight inches in diameter at the stump. I chopped it down and cut off all the limbs, then chopped a foot long section off one end. We forced it under the leaf springs right next to the axle and then into the ground, using it as a wedge. First, we backed the truck up onto this, and it raised the axle up about four inches. I chopped off another piece, placed it on the opposite side of the axle and moved the truck forward this time. This raised the axle high enough for us to place the bottle jack under the axle and change the tire. Before dropping the truck back down we filled the muddy ditch with rocks and branches. We were back in business, and ready to go after the dead lion. We were only a few hundred feet from the end of the road, which is where the old mine was. I was looking in plain sight of the abandoned cabins, when out of nowhere two young boys walked out onto the road leading four hound dogs. From the direction they were coming from, it looked as if they had followed me down to where we were. They introduced themselves as Gary and Bobby, and I asked where they had come from and what were they doing. These two boys, who looked to be about the same age as Roy, said they were bear hunting with their father, who had turned them loose at Rhymes Camp, about two miles away. Their plan was that they would walk the dogs through the woods and hopefully they would get after a bear, or better yet a lion. In the mean-time their dad would drive around and pick them up somewhere nearby. They went on to tell us that, two days earlier they had caught a very large bear in Wagy Flats. They said that they and their dad had packed it out all in one piece and took it to the truck scale in Lake Isabella where it weighed in at 441 pounds, field dressed. I thought, *Really*? It was easy to see that they were both well conditioned, without a lazy bone in their bodies. But I found it hard to believe that Gary, who was sixteen, and his brother Bobby, who was only fourteen, had packed out a bear of that size with their father, and all in one piece. These seemed to be some pretty good kids, and they went on to tell us that they were from Shasta County California, and their dad was a logging contractor, who had a timber contract in the area. They were now temporarily staying in Lake Isabella, and would be there until they finished their contract here. I liked both of them and wanted to meet their dad.

I then made a proposition. I told them that we had a dead lion down at the bottom of that canyon and I said that if they would agree to help us get it out, that I would load them up, dogs and all, and together we would find their dad. They gladly accepted the offer. The four of us went down to the lion where we tied it onto a long limb that could be carried out with one person on each end.

We had only gone about a hundred feet when one of the boys asked if it would be okay with me if we stopped what we were doing and let them carry it out on their backs, one at a time. Well, I said, if that's what you wanted to try, okay, have at it. The lion was no lightweight, probably 135 pounds, and the canyon wall was at about a forty-five degree angle, and as I said before the road was close to a quarter mile away. Gary wanted to go first, so he kneeled down while we all helped put the dead lion over his shoulders and we helped him stand up. Then Gary said, "Okay, let's go"! Off he went, then after he went about one-hundred yards, he dropped and Bobby loaded it onto his shoulders, and off he went. These kids were like a steam powered locomotive. They traded this lion back and forth a few more times and next thing I knew we were all standing in the road.

I couldn't help but compliment them both on what I had just witnessed, and they both said at the same time, "This was nothing compared to what we've seen our Dad do." After seeing that, their story about hauling a 441 pound bear out of the woods began to sound believable.

From there, we loaded up the dead lion, all of our dogs, and the four of us crammed ourselves into the cab of my truck and off we went. As we were heading up the road to find their dad, Gary mentioned to me to watch out for his dad, he said that when he's looking for them he is almost always driving pretty fast. He had no sooner got that out and there he was, breaks locked up and skidding to a stop.

December 1966
Jim Bridges
Lake Isabella, CA

Many times I have looked back at the coincidence of this meeting, because without the flat tire, I would have never met them and their Dad,

Jim. I also had no idea that this meeting would eventually bring a lasting friendship between Jim, Gary and me. Jim and I joined forces for two years on guiding bear hunts throughout Northern California. We also hunted together for a short time in Nevada, but because we lived so far from each other, we eventually went our separate ways.

Eventually, I ended up buying three of the four hounds that they had with them that day. First was Liz, a Black and Tan, next Spot, a Walker, and last but not least was Flipper, who was a Bluetick. All three of these hounds were outstanding bear dogs, and when added to the dogs I already had, they gave me an outstanding pack for hunting bears, lions, and bobcats.

About this same time my advertising started paying off, and I started to get more paying hunters. Then, in the following early spring I picked up a three–month-old female Bluetick hound from a guy who lived in the Ventura area. He didn't hunt, just liked the breed and had a small litter of Bluetick pups. This pup was of the Elbert Vaughn breeding, which I was very familiar with, and I had even hunted with some of her close relatives when I was in Arkansas and Mississippi. All of them were very good dogs. I named her "Lil".

Then in the late fall of '67 when I received a phone call from a friend of mine, Russ Larson, who was in the process of building a subdivision at Sugarloaf Village, in the Sequoia National Forest. He told me he had received a call from a friend of his, Dewy Linze, a writer for the Los Angeles Times. Dewy had apparently seen my advertising, asked Russ if he knew me, and wanted to know if he thought I would be interested in taking him on a lion hunt. He went on to explain that if all went well they would publish a story about it in the Los Angeles Times, Sunday Edition. The Times thought the story would be interesting to their readers, since it was happening so close to the Los Angeles area, and Dewy really wanted to go on a lion hunt. At first, I thought he was kidding, but he said it was no joke, so we went about setting it up. The newspaper would only allow four days for the trip, and everything had to be all on their terms, including the dates.

I had another hunter scheduled around the same time that Dewy wanted to be here, and I was concerned about having these two hunts so close together. First came the bow hunter and he got what he wanted on his second day. It was a good-sized male lion. He took it and went on his way. I was happy that this got over quick, because it would give me about a week before Dewy was scheduled to arrive and I hoped I could find another lion by then. I looked everywhere, but had no luck finding any sign, and that worried me a little. I thought it was pretty important for the hunt to be successful. But I'd just have to wait to see what happened after they got there.

Russ called me as soon as they arrived at his house, and the next morning I was introduced to Dewy and the photographer, J. Berry Herron was a freelancer who worked primarily for National Geographic, and mainly as an underwater photographer. To say I was impressed would be an understatement. I could hardly believe it. A National Geographic Photographer and a Los Angeles Times reporter were actually there to hunt with me. This was a very important hunt for me, and there was no way that I could send them home empty-handed. It looked like it was going to be all bare ground trailing conditions, which was going to make it much more difficult than if there were snow on the ground. But that was okay because almost all the lions that I caught here were caught in the same conditions. I only had four days to get it done, and four days is not much time to do this on bare ground. All I needed was to find one track fresh enough for Bo and Saylor and they would do the rest.

We started hunting in the Alder Creek area on the first day, but with no luck. On the second day we tried the White River area and it was the same thing. The next day I took them to the McFarland Creek area and it was early in the morning when I found it: a female lion track. Not a very large one, but it was a lion. It crossed the road coming from below, close to the area where I once lived in the old trailer where the landlord didn't want me to hunt on his land. First, I tried Bo on it to see what he did, and it was good, so I let Saylor and Lil out with him. The track wasn't smoking hot, but it was good enough. From there it went up towards Bohna Peak, turned to the north and headed towards McFarland Creek, crossed both forks there, and then headed towards the old Munn Camp site. The trailing was slow at first but once they had gone about a quarter mile, the conditions got better and the next thing we knew the dogs had it jumped and running. They treed the lion in a Live Oak that was just above the road that we were traveling on, and about one mile from where we started. The entire race was fast and only took the dogs about an hour from start to finish. Once we got to the tree, the lion saw us coming and jumped out and headed downhill as fast as it could run. But that only lasted for about two minutes before the dogs had it up another tree. This time it was even closer to the road than the first time, which was going to make it easier for us when it came to packing it out to the truck.

Dewy got the lion he was wanting, Berry got his photos for the newspaper, and I ended up with a four page, full color article in the West Magazine, Sunday Edition of the Los Angeles Times Newspaper.

Having these two on a hunt with me was a break that I never thought I would be getting and it, in time, helped in boosting my business.

1968
Summertime in Bull Run Basin

Here is a male California lion of average size, about fifty feet up in a large Yellow Pine that was along the Western edge of Bull Run Basin, in Sequoia National Forest. So, what was he thinking? It's hard to say. It looked to me that he was just watching to see what I'm up to. I caught him on a hot August day in 1969. Even though the lions in California were still not protected at the time, I didn't kill all that I caught, including this one. We caught him and that was good enough for me, so after a few minutes of praising my dogs, I leashed them up and let him go on his way, unharmed. I was pretty good at identifying animal tracks, and most of the time I could tell if I had seen a particular lion or bear track before. When it came to this one, I don't think that I ever saw any sign of him again. Not everyone that lived in this part of the country went along with my ideas of letting lions go free, especially ranchers and deer hunters who looked at the lion as the worst thing that ever walked through these mountains. I will admit, some of them can get pretty rough, so letting a lion go free was not always a popular thing to do. On the other hand, there is only one way to deal with lions that start killing domestic animals, and that is to hunt them down and kill them as quickly as possible. Personally, I had no vendetta against any of the animals that I hunted, I just liked hunting with my dogs and if I had a paying customer, and if the season was open, have at it. To the best of my knowledge, I was the only one around there who would do something like this. When it came to the lions killing deer? That didn't bother me either; they were only doing what they were created to do.

1968

As sub species go, California has the second largest Mountain Lions, with the Rocky Mountain States being the largest. Here are two good size lions, male on the right and female on the left. Both were taken in the Greenhorn Mountains. They were caught separately and within three days of each other. Photo is in front of the old Panorama Heights Lodge, Posey, CA.

There were many good-sized bears like this one around when they started showing up again in the Greenhorn Mountains. This made me believe that these were migrating in from someplace else, such as the National Park to the North.

As you can see here, the Greenhorns Mountains produced more than just good lion hunting; it also produced bears, and some pretty-good sized ones at that. Here is an example of a large bear. This one was killed at the head of Scarlet and Davis Canyon, about 7,500 ft. in elevation. It was late December and with over one foot of snow on the ground, we were able to put it on a toboggan and drag it half a mile down the main road. From there we went to the sawmill at Johnsondale, where it weighed in at 397 pounds, field dressed. After butchering, it rendered twenty-plus gallons of lard. Packing out large bears like this one, and in one piece isn't always possible, leaving their weight to only guessing.

There were other places I hunted that definitely had larger concentrations of bears than in the Greenhorns, but from 1970, and on there were enough here to keep me satisfied, at least until the change in hunting regulations made it impossible for me to make a living anymore.

Here is an extra large black bear, treed in an extra large Sugar Pine tree. I believe he was at least 100 plus feet above the ground. I couldn't see him in the tree when standing at the bottom of it, and in order to get this picture, I needed to climb up the mountainside to where I was almost level to him, and by then I needed a 125-mm. telephoto lens. After taking this, I snapped up the dogs and said goodbye. I don't think I ever saw him again.

Pictured here is something that every bear hunter wants to find. The back foot, shown here, measured ten inches in length, while the front foot measured a solid six inches wide. This photo was taken in my driveway in the Greenhorn Mountains, summer of 1995.

I would like to point out here that what the bears in the Greenhorn Mountains lacked in numbers, they were able to make up for it in size, and when it came to guiding, this was always a plus for my hunters.

Chapter 7

PEEL MILL CREEK

By the winter of 1967, I had been hunting in the Greenhorn Mountains around Glennville for about four years, and had lived in the area for a little over a year. During that time, I had learned quite a bit about that part of the Greenhorns, the most important was learning where the best places were at to find any lions. One of those places was Sandy Creek Fire Road. This road cut across the mountains on the western side of Sunday Peak. It was about thirteen miles long and travelled north to south at about the 5,000 feet in elevation, all within the Sequoia National Forest. If there were any lions in the area, they would almost always cross that road.

I had caught several lions there so far this year, and one morning I decided to go again and take a look. At the time there wasn't any snow at that elevation. Plus, it hadn't rained for about a week and the dirt was beginning to harden up, so finding tracks on the bare ground was not going to be easy. I entered the southern end of the road, and at first I turned only Bo loose to hunt in front of the truck, and after we had traveled about a mile, Bo started to show some interest, as though something had been there, but he wasn't too sure of what it was. Bo was looking and trying real hard to find out whatever it was, but there just wasn't enough scent for him to actually trail it. At that particular spot the dirt was almost rock hard and there was no way that I could see what he was trying to trail, so just the two of us started walking the road together, with Bo looking for scent, while I looked for tracks.

The two of us walked together for about a quarter mile, and when we got about a few hundred feet from where the road crosses over McFarland. Creek, I found one track of a lion. It was made in the mud while the road was still wet, so that put it at least four days old. I got Bo over to where I could point it out, to see if he could smell anything, and after he stuck his nose deep into the track, his tail started wagging real fast, and he let out a howl, which let me know he smelled it. It was nothing the dogs could trail, but it was a start, and now we both knew that there was a lion somewhere in the area. So, we started moving forward in the direction that it seemed to be going.

The next time I found its tracks was where it had come down into the road from above, just a little north of McFarland Creek, and from there it followed the road to a place called Munn Camp. I could see some tracks, or parts of a foot print now and then, so I let Saylor out with Bo to see if he could help, and together these two were able to get a whiff of it every now and then, but it was still too old for them to be able to trail it. Now it was the three of us looking for any sign of where it went, and the last I could see anything was where it left the road, and was heading down hill toward an area better known as Bear Dens. Although it appeared to have been there within the last few days, the dogs could only catch a whiff from one place or another. I knew it had to be somewhere in the area and it looked to me as though it was hunting both sides of the road, as it continued traveling north.

I kept looking along the sides of the road for any tracks, and then, just as we started to round the bend in the road and go into Sandy Creek, I saw where it had come back up onto the road, where it continued heading north for about half a mile. It stayed walking on the road until it crossed over Sandy Creek and from there it left the road and headed up onto the south side of Telephone Ridge. At that point the dogs were able to pick up its scent better than before, but still not good enough to trail it. So, I put the dogs back into the truck and drove another half mile to where the road crossed Telephone Ridge, looking for tracks all the way into Peel Mill Creek. But we found nothing.

I had now gone about seven miles from where I first saw any sign of the lion. At the beginning, the dogs could barely catch any of its scent, and now, from the way the dogs reacted when they were trying to trail it, it appeared as though we could be less than twenty-four hours behind it, so we're getting closer. I found no sign of any thing being killed, and if that was the case, then it had not had anything to eat for some time. It could be taking its time while it hunted, and there were quite a few deer in the area, so my guess was that it would stick around and hunt there for a while, or at least that is what I was hoping for. By now it was late afternoon, and I decided to load up and head for home. I was sure that this lion was somewhere close by, and maybe closer than one would think. Now it's a guessing game, and I need to give it some time to move around. I'll be back in the morning and maybe then I can pick up the trail. From what I had seen so far, this lion was staying close to the same elevation where I first found its tracks. I had followed it for about nine miles, and I am expecting that it will stay close to that elevation for some time. Tomorrow I'm going to try and get out in front of it. I want to see if I can meet it head on.

As soon as I got home I made a phone call to a friend I had hunted with many times before. Joe Bryan, he was always a very good hand to have around when hunting; he knew how to handle the dogs, would look and help find tracks, and he also had helped me to live capture lions before. Joe worked for the Kern County Fire Department, and if he had time off to go, he would be there. I told Joe what I had found and he was game. He lived only about eight miles from where we were going to go. When I picked him up he mentioned that there was a new owner at the Jack Ranch Resort named Pete who would like to go along as well. We picked Pete up on our way, and headed to the north end of the Sandy Creek Fire Road.

I told them where I had last seen the lion's tracks the day before and said, today we will be coming in from the north end of the road and head toward Telephone Ridge. My plan was to keep the dogs in the truck until we got close to Peel Mill Creek, where I would start looking for any tracks in the road, and then let Bo and Saylor out to hunt from there. When we were about a half-mile from where the creek crossed the road, the dogs caught scent of something, and they all started barking and wanted out of the truck. It wasn't unusual for them to do something like this if it was a bear that had crossed the road, but there were no bears out at that time of the year. I got out to look for any tracks that might be in the road, but just like the day before it was rock hard and impossible to see any tracks. All the while the dogs were going nuts and wanting out, so all I could do now was turn them loose and find out what was going on.

First, I let Bo and Saylor out and they took off running as hard as they could go. Then, I let Lil, Thunder and Liz out right behind them and off they went. They crossed Peel Mill Creek in a dead run, and headed up the north side of Telephone Ridge, and within only a few minutes they were treed. That was as fast and easy as it gets. They had treed within five hundred feet of the road. We had no idea of what they had caught until we arrived at the tree, and there it was. This lion must have met us head on in the road as we were coming up, and when it either saw or heard us, it ran down into the canyon below, then ran up about a quarter mile up Telephone Ridge and treed. It was treed up a large black oak that had a good lean to it. It would have been easy to put a noose around its neck, but it had treed so easily that the dogs didn't get much of a run, so I wanted to jump it out and let the dogs tree it again. I found a branch that was about ten feet long, climbed up to within ten feet of the lion and just as I started waving the stick around its face, it jumped out and the race was back on.

Down the canyon they went and in a dead run, crossing Peel Mill Creek again and running parallel to the road that we had just come up. Then, as they started running up out of the canyon, and heading to the north towards the road, they treed it again. This time it went up a large

White Fir tree that was about a hundred feet below the road. At one time this tree had been hit by lightning, which knocked the top off, about forty feet up, and another top had grown out of the fracture, and that's exactly where the lion was sitting when we first got there. It was an average-sized female lion, and since I didn't have any lion hunts lined up for some time, and my lion cage at home was empty, I thought this would be a great opportunity to take this one home alive, plus it wasn't often that I had any help to do this, and I knew I could count on Joe.

I had not started using tranquilizers yet to help with this, so it was going to be done the old-fashioned way: no drugs, just ropes. We had nothing but time, so why not? As usual, I had my cables and ropes with me, plus lions that were her size were easier to handle than trying to do this with an old tom lion, so here we go. First, we needed to get it out of this tree and into another one that we could climb. There was no way we could get a noose around its neck with it that far up in this tree. So, we started throwing rocks and sticks at it in hopes it would jump out and go up another tree somewhere else where the ground wasn't as steep, and the tree wasn't as tall. This wasn't working at all, in fact we couldn't believe it, but after about five minutes of throwing everything we could find small enough to throw, it laid itself down, and looked like it had fallen asleep. Then Joe said, the only way we'll ever get this lion out of this tree would be to cut the tree down. Well, I had never done anything like that before, but I thought, why not? I always carried a chainsaw in my truck, so I went and got it. I knew that Joe was pretty good at felling trees in the right direction and the plan was that since the hillside was very steep, he would drop it uphill. Doing this, it wouldn't have to fall very far and maybe the lion would jump out before it hit the ground, and ahead of the tree, and hopefully everything would turn out okay.

In the meantime, Pete was standing above us, and a little below the road, giving himself plenty of room to avoid being hit by the tree when it fell. We knew there were risks involved in what we were doing, but we were on a mission. Hopefully, the lion wouldn't get hurt in the fall. We even hoped that the sound of the chainsaw might scare it out of the tree, but that didn't work. This lion was so comfortable right where it was, that it almost slept through everything.

Well, almost everything.

First, Joe cut the notch on the uphill side of the tree, so it would fall in that direction, and the lion didn't pay any attention. But after Joe started cutting on the opposite side and when the tree began to shake a little, it woke up, raised its head and opened its eyes wide open. Then, as the tree started to fall, the lion pulled back on its front legs as though it was trying to stop the ground from coming at it. Just as the tree was about a third of the way down, it jumped and hit the ground just a little ahead of the tree. With the tree right behind it and coming fast, the lion made a short run uphill, almost running into Pete, whose eyes were wide open. Then it made a quick about face and ran right past the tree as it was hitting the ground, and at the same time I turned the dogs loose again. It ran down the mountainside as fast as it could, with the dogs right along beside it. This now looked more like a stamped than anything else. As far as we could see, and as soon as they hit the bottom it treed again.

While we were standing there watching this, Pete told us we were both crazy, as he climbed the mountain and disappeared up onto the road. I guess all of it was just too much for him and he was on his way home, alone. Joe and I hurried down to the hounds and the lion, and the situation had improved a little, we were on flatter ground and the lion was only about twenty feet up in a small fir tree. But the limbs were so thick and tangled together that we couldn't get a noose through the branches. Joe asked me what I thought we should do? I saw that he still had the chainsaw with him, so I thought about it for maybe two seconds, then I told him to fire up the chainsaw again. Joe started cutting away, and this time the lion was paying attention. Letting this lion go free was no longer an option. As the tree with the lion in it fell into the creek along with a mixture of falling timber and brush, we were unable to see where the lion was. Thinking that the lion had run off again as the tree fell, I turned the dogs loose, only to find that it was in the creek and that was where it had made up its mind to take a stand against us. This wasn't exactly what we had planned on, but it was what we had to deal with.

All of a sudden, we had one huge pile of brush with the lion, and five dogs all together, and right in the middle of Peel Mill Creek. The Creek was about five feet wide and two to three feet deep and completely surrounded in by dense scrub brush, not counting the tree that we just cut down. The dogs had the lion surrounded and were going crazy trying to get at it, which kept it occupied and prevented it from running away, it was easy to see if this lion got ahold of anyone of these dogs while in all of this brush, and limbs, there would be no way anyone could save it from being killed. I immediately handed the noose over to Joe, and started grabbing up dogs as fast as I could get my hands on them and tied them to anything I could find. In the meantime Joe, who incidentally had never done anything like this, opened up an area through the brush where he could try to get close enough to get the noose over the lion's head. The clearing he made was kind of small, and it looked like he was standing right in the middle of the only exit the lion could use if it wanted out. At the same time we were both ready to shoot it if it tried to get ahold of either one of us or the dogs. The next thing I knew Joe had opened up an area where he could get close enough, and he started attaching the cabled and noose to the end of a six to eight foot stick. Then with outstretched arms, which put him within eight feet of the lion's head, Joe began dangling the noose in front of the lions head.

As usual with most lions, she started to hiss and tried to bluff Joe away as he approached with the noose. Joe took his time as he moved closer, and within a few minutes, he was able to put the noose over her head and we were in business. By then I had caught up all of the dogs, and as Joe began pulling it towards him, I snuck behind it, grabbing its tail, then I got a small rope around one of its back feet, put a half hitch over the other one and we had it.

I found a short piece of an oak limb, put it into her mouth, attached some bailing wire to it and wrapped that around her head so she couldn't bite us. We then tied her front and back feet together, so all I needed now was my horse to help pack it out. I had to leave Joe there with the dogs and lion while I went back to Glennville, which meant I would be gone for about an hour and a half.

It was about nine miles from where I left Joe, to Jack Ranch, and just as I was approaching it, I caught up with Pete. He was still walking down the road, and only a few hundred feet from entering his driveway. I pulled up next to him, asked how he was doing, and offered him a ride the rest of the way, but he just kept walking. As I tried to explain everything to him, he assured me once again that both Joe and I were totally insane, thanked me for taking him with us, then quickly disappeared down his driveway.

I continued heading for home, grabbed everything that we would need, loaded my horse into the back of the truck, and got back just as the sun was setting and it went dark. When I got out of the truck, I noticed that there were no dogs barking. So, I hollered down into the canyon to Joe, and found that he wasn't far and had all of the dogs with him. I waited until he got to the road to talk and see what had happened. He told me, that shortly after I left him, he had started a small fire about thirty feet away from the lion, to keep warm and provide himself with some light. He went on to say that everything seemed to be going just fine, but then about thirty minutes later, the lion started thrashing around a little bit, closed its eyes and died. "From what?" I asked. "I don't know," he said, "it just died." It wasn't at all what we wanted to have happen, but, I must admit, we had put that thing through a pretty rough time. So, now we're going to do a little autopsy on it as soon as we got it out of here.

We loaded it onto my horse and headed out and on to Joe's house where we opened it up to see if there were any internal injuries, then we skinned it out. It was there that we found it had broken a rib that had punctured a lung, and that was why it died. True enough, it was all my fault for trying to do anything like that, and unfortunately, there would be a few more accidents like it before I learned what to do and what not to do when taking a lion alive, especially without the aid of tranquilizers. Like so many other things, there's usually a learning curve involved in the process of trying to get things right or even to obtain perfection. Like most everything else, I had to learn it on my own. But this was only the second and last lion that I accidently killed while trying to do a live capture without using any tranquilizers.

Shortly after that I was able to purchase a tranquilizer gun from the local rancher supply store in Glennville. But this had its own dangers; without a veterinarian prescribed drug it could be just as lethal. At the time the only drug that was available to me was one called Cap-Chur Sol, which was actually a derivative of nicotine. When administered, I had to be right about the animal's weight, because if I gave the animal just a little over on the recommended dosage, it would die, and if I underestimated, it wouldn't stay down. This tranquilizer was designed to immobilize everything from wild dogs to mean bulls. I would use it at times, but only in small doses, and then only to slow a lion down enough to get the noose over its head. It wasn't until years later, when I began helping with the mountain lion research program for the Montana Game & Fish Department that I had anything to use that would be considered safe for sedating the lions, and even that wasn't foolproof.

1967

Joe Bryan

Somewhere along the White River Road in Tulare County

Chapter 8

THE RINCON TRAIL

It was at the end of February 1968, and I had taken a few lions out of the Glennville area in the past few weeks and I wanted to make a run over to the Kern River area to check out things there. This time I would be hunting on the Rincon Trail, just north of the Sherman Pass Road. I liked hunting there, since there wasn't many other hound hunters who used it, and I could usually count on finding some lion activity in certain areas during the winter months. It was pretty good horse country, so I would be taking my horse along with me. Because of the long drive to get there, I would also take my camp trailer, and set up camp somewhere close to where I was planning to hunt. I left Glennville at about four in the morning. The drive going over Greenhorn Summit would usually take me about two and a half to three hours when loaded, with my horse in the back of my truck and pulling my camp trailer, so leaving early in the morning was a must if I was planning to hunt the same day. Therefore, on this day I had everything loaded and was on the road by 3:30 that morning. It was about 6 a.m. when I arrived at my usual camping site, which was along the east side of the Kern River and at the junction of Sherman Peak Road. It didn't take long for me to set up camp since, all I had to do was unhook my camp trailer and drive away with my horse and dogs both in the back of my truck. At the time, the Sherman

Pass road was closed so I would have to ride on horseback starting from the Kern river for about two and a half miles, and from there I would connect with the Rincon trail and head North. It was from that point on that I expected to find some lion signs.

All of the snow at the elevation where we were headed was gone, with the exception of what was on the north slopes, and with the nighttime temperatures dropping to well below freezing, the ground was frozen and hard as a brick. If the days warmed up enough, the ground in the open areas would thaw out enough to where tracks that were left by heavier animals could be found. Otherwise, I had to rely on my dogs to find the right tracks on their own. As soon as I started out on my horse, I let Saylor loose to find tracks, while I hooked my other four dogs together in pairs to follow. We had only gone about two and a half miles towards Durrwood Creek when Saylor struck a track on the upper side of the trail, but from the sound of his voice I didn't think he was smelling a lion. Judging from the way he was barking I figured it had to be a bobcat. This was not what I wanted to hunt, but there was no stopping him, so I turned Liz, Spot, Bonnie, and Thunder loose to join in, and before they could get to him, he had it up a tree. What just happened here was no surprise to me, because if it was a bobcat, Saylor would have it up a tree within a couple of minutes once he jumped it. I was able to ride my horse right to them, and sure enough, it was a bobcat. I had no reason to kill it, so I hooked up all the dogs and lead them away, letting the cat go free. Once I knew they wouldn't go back to the bobcat, I turned Saylor loose again and continued riding north.

I had gone about another mile when I heard Saylor strike another trail; once again he struck another track to the east, and about five hundred feet above me. This time he sounded different. This time he had a lot more excitement in his voice, which usually indicated he was onto the scent of a lion. As I've mentioned, with the ground so bare and frozen, there was no telling what it was and I had to leave it to the dogs. Judging from the way he was working this track, it sounded to me like it was a lion, and not that old of a track. So, I turned all of the others loose and within seconds they were all with Saylor.

After about five minutes of cold trailing, they started picking up speed. They hadn't jumped it, but they were now moving out at a pretty good pace. They continued trailing around the west side of Sherman Peak and the farther they went the faster they ran. I continued to move along in the direction they were going, but remaining about a quarter mile below and behind them. I was doing my best to make sure they didn't get out of hearing, and at the same time I wanted to stay on my horse. They were now about 1000 feet in elevation above me, and still climbing, then they headed north at full speed. They were now heading into the upper portion of Durrwood Creek, and just about out of hearing. I immediately turned my horse around and headed back to the Rincon Trail and then headed north to where it crossed Durrwood Creek, from there I rode straight up the north side of the main canyon. After riding about a quarter mile I started hearing the dogs again, and this time they were treeing. From there I rode on my horse right to the tree.

Well, there he was. About twenty feet above the ground, in a small Bull Pine tree that was only about thirty feet tall. At first glance as I rode up, I could tell that he was a good sized male lion. Right off, I tied up my horse to a nearby tree, and then as I walked a little closer to the tree, I could see that this lion was much larger than anything I had expected to see in this area. In fact, the more that I looked at him, the bigger he looked. I couldn't help but wonder, where did this guy come from. Then I remembered my friend, Johnny McNally telling me about a lion that Howard Bilton had seen tracks of. Howard told about a lion that lived in this area, and he said that it was by far the largest lion track he had ever seen. Could this be him? If it is him, then he would have to be at least 11 or more years old. As I walked around this tree I could tell that he was the largest lion that I had ever seen (or ever *will* see, for that matter) in California. Statistics at the time put the average male lion in California at somewhere between 120 to 125 pounds with the larger ones weighing in at 135 pounds or slightly more. It was hard for me to give an accurate estimate of his weight since I had never put any lion of his size on a scale, however, this guy had to tip the scales at something over 165 pounds, and that would be on an empty stomach. He actually looked a lot more like some of the larger males that live in the Rocky Mountains.

As usual, the dogs were all fired up and happy to see me, while this lion simply watched, calm and indifferent. I tied my horse to a nearby tree to make sure he was out of the way and tied each dog to anything that would hold them in case something went wrong. I had no camera with me, and no intention of me killing him for myself, but then I didn't really want to simply let him go free either. Again, I started looking him over and trying to decide if I could take him alive. I had live captured several lions before but none nearly as large as this one, so I knew I needed to think it over very carefully before I started anything. I always carried my live capture equipment with me, which wasn't much more than a few ropes, a quarter inch wire cable made into a noose, bailing wire and some duct tape. But for this to work out, I would first have to get him onto the ground. Then, after he settled down, I'd need to try and get a rope onto one of his back legs and from there I could sort of stretch him out and then finish tying him up and tie him across the saddle on my horse, and away we could go.

He was too far above the ground for me to get a rope around him without climbing up a nearby tree to get closer. If I tried that I'd be able to get closer and then get a noose around his head and neck, climb back down to the ground and pull him out. If I couldn't catch him off balance, or if he was simply too strong for me do it on my own, I could dally the rope to my saddle horn and pull him out with my horse. I had done this before, so I knew it could work.

I also needed to find a good straight stick about eight feet long to attach the rope and noose to the end of it. I found just what I needed, assembled the rig, and then climbed a tree that was next to the one he was in without any problems. I was now less than ten feet from him, and about twenty feet off the ground. All the while I was doing this, I noticed that this old lion had been watching every move I made from the time I arrived and unlike any others, all he did was watch me. When I first started climbing up to get closer to him he was standing on two limbs, front feet on one and his hind feet on another, with his body leaning against the trunk of the tree. Then, as I got closer, he started to lower his body into a crouched position, and watching every move that I made. It was easy to see that he was engrossed in every move that I made. Once I got to his level and looked directly at him, I could see that his eyes were already locked directly onto mine. Unlike any other lion I'd done this with, there was no hissing, no growling, no bluffing, or no sign of fear. When I started to approach him with the cable and noose, he didn't pay any attention to that either. I'm sure that he could see this stick with a noose hanging off the end of it as it was not only waving in front of his face, it was also touching him. But he acted as though there was nothing there. Instead he was busy reading my every thought. It was now easy to see that he wasn't one bit afraid of me. Then I could see that as he was tightening up the muscles in his legs and feet, he was pulling his ears back tightly against his neck. With his mouth tightly closed, he slowly started to inch his way toward me. It all seemed so fluid and automatic; it was like his body was being controlled by his subconscious. This surprised me—all the others would pull back and look for a way out, but not him. He never even blinked; he meant business, no doubt about it. I either stopped what I was doing, and get out of that tree right now, or he was coming over. So what was stopping him? I knew what he was wanting to do!

The only thing that I could think of was that he was waiting for me to look away, and I wasn't about to do anything like that, at least not with him so close to me. It was hard to figure why animals like him would ever run away from the dogs instead of running them down and killing them. You take a lion of his size, who was easily three times the size of the largest dog there, and built to kill animals much larger than them, I would think that he could have easily killed all of them. But he didn't. Instead, he did like most lions do, and climbed a tree. But this time, in his mind he has met his biggest adversary, one that wanted to fight him no matter where he went.

He's ready to start defending himself, and that meant getting rid of me. But first, he needed to figure out how to go about it. At this point I knew that I didn't dare look away from him or even blink. I definitely couldn't show any sign of being afraid of him. That could have been all he needed. So, I carefully pulled back the stick and noose that was dangling in his face, then very slowly took my right hand off of the stick, and I pulled my revolver part way out of its holster. Without losing eye contact, and for the next few seconds neither of us moved, and continued looking directly into each other's eyes. Then very slowly I stopped what I had been doing, and started to move away from him, and at the same time he stopped.

He had sized me up as something that he has had enough of, and I had done the same with him. It was time for me to let him go. Or was it him that was letting *me* go? I wasn't sure, but without moving too fast, I began climbing back down the tree. I have to admit; he was something special to look at, especially being so close, and with nothing but air between the two of us. He appeared to be very old and battle-scarred from head to tail, dark gray in color, with splits and pieces missing on both ears. I never took my eyes off him as I climbed down the tree. He did the same, and by the time I was halfway down I could see he had pushed his ears back into their normal upright position, which was a relief. There was no doubt in my mind, he wouldn't have gone down without a fight and it was no doubt a fight. All the while this was going on, my dogs were barking as hard and loud as they could, but that didn't seem to bother him anymore. All he saw was me. The moment I got back onto the ground I rounded up my dogs and got on my horse. As I rode away, I looked back at him, kind of smiled to myself, tipped my hat out of respect, and under my breath I whispered to myself, "I'll be back." All the while admitting to myself that it was probably a good thing I didn't get that noose over his head.

On my way home, I stopped at Johnny McNally's Restaurant and told John the story. Boy, did that light a fire under him! He couldn't understand why anyone would do what I had just done. He went on to tell me that this had to be the same lion that Howard Bilton told him about some ten years earlier, only he had never got close enough to catch him. Well, I agree, with Howard Bilton. If this is the same lion that he was talking about, he was not only big, I will also add, special. John then proceeded to tell me about all the damage that lions had done throughout the centuries and how my letting that particular one go free had to be the worst thing he had ever heard. Clearly, we didn't share the same opinions, but we remained good friends just the same.

According to John there were a few others who had seen this lions tracks before, and they all were impressed by the extra large foot print that he left behind him as he walked along. I had never heard any of these stories before, so when I caught him I was not expecting that there was any lions in this part of the country that could be so big.

Whether this was him or not, he was very old, and very big, At that time, I looked at him as just another lion, but down inside of me, I'm sure that he was the one that Howard talked about.

Putting all of that aside, this I know for sure; he was by far the largest lion that I ever caught in California, very old, covered with battle scars from one end to the other, and wasn't one bit afraid of me. Plus, I am sure that I am the only one to have ever locked eyes with him in a nose to nose standoff, and a standoff where we each let the other go free.

Myself in the saddle, with Spot hunting in front of us.

This is where I would usually start my ride as I headed North along the Rincon trail. In the far horizon, you can see an outcropping of large rocks known as the Needles. The Needles are on the opposite side of the Kern river, and this trail. They are also about three air miles directly to the east from where I treed the old tom lion that I told about in this story.

When I had no hunters to guide for lions, or in between hunts, I still needed to stay on top of where there were lions. This meant that I needed to keep on the move, looking and trying to find them. While doing this I had to keep in mind that it didn't do me much good to find lions in places where it was to difficult to take the majority of paying customers. Because of this, there were large portions of good lion country that I eliminated. When hunting alone on the Rincon Trail, my goal was to ride in as far as possible, then turn around and ride back out, all on the same day. From my camping spot on the Kern River to the Forks of the Kern was about 13 miles each way (as the crow fly's).

This was all good lion country during the winter months, as long as the deer were here, there would be lions somewhere in there with them. Still, it was big country, and just because they could be in there, didn't mean it would be easy to find them

Chapter 9

JOHNSONDALE

After leaving the Rincon Trail I returned home to Glennville, and since I knew I was coming back within a week, I left my trailer there. This gave my dogs and me some much-needed time to rest up. I had a client coming in for a lion hunt in less than a week, and I also wanted to do some scouting for lion signs a little closer to home and hunt there if possible. I had no luck in finding any activity there. When my hunting client from Los Angeles arrived, we loaded everything up, and headed back to Johnsondale,

I told this guy about what I had been doing lately, which included treeing and letting go the extra-large male lion that I had caught on the Rincon Trail only days earlier. As soon as I mentioned its size, he immediately said this was the lion he wanted to claim for himself, and was willing to do whatever it took to get him. So off we went. The weather had changed right after I left, making the daytime temperatures very comfortable, however, the nights remained quite cold and stayed below freezing. There was very little snow except for places that were shaded or on the northern slopes, and most of that had a hard crust of ice over the top of it and only the heaviest animals would break through it. As a result, it was the same as it was the week before, I would have to rely on the dogs to search out and find any lion tracks.

My new client was a nice guy, said he hunted a lot, was in the best of shape, could go forever on foot, and didn't need anyone looking after him. He went on to tell me the only reason he was hiring me was that he didn't have any lion dogs of his own, otherwise he would have been doing this by himself. I had never heard anyone put it to me quite like that before, but this all sounded good to me, so first thing at daybreak we saddled up the horses and off we went onto the Rincon Trail. Saylor was still my lead dog, and he would be the only one loose to scout for tracks while the others were snapped together and stayed by our horses. We rode from sunup until about noon, and then we ran into the crusted snow that was still about knee deep on the northern slopes, making it hard for the horses to get through. I decided it would be best if we tied them up and went on foot from there. I really wanted to see if there was any sign of the big tom or any other lions in the area. When we first took off, I told him to remember that for every mile we went in, it was the same mile that we would have to cover coming back, so if he tired, I needed him to let me know.

We were just past Durrwood Creek, or about nine miles in, when we left the horses, and I wanted to go at least another four miles before calling it a day. This would have put us close to the forks of the Kern River. That would make it an eight-mile round trip on foot, plus another nine miles on horseback. We would travel a combined total of twenty-six miles, but who knows, something could cross our trail behind us. Before leaving our horses, we had downed our lunch, and this guy still looked to be okay. Everything seemed fine, only, there was no sign of any lions. Then after about two miles of hiking he said he needed to stop and rest for a while, which that was fine with me. It was now about 3 PM and I suggested that he could stay there for about an hour while I went on ahead to check for tracks. I went on for about a mile or so, didn't see any tracks, then returned as promised and suggested that we start heading back. The sun was starting to cast heavy shadows over most of the area and in some places the ground was starting to freeze up again. Then out of nowhere, he starts telling me that he wanted to spend the night, right there! He wants to sleep on the frozen ground, without any shelter or food. He went on to say that we could head out in the morning after sunup, get the horses, and continue our hunt for a lion on our way back.

He went on to explain that he hadn't realized how far we had come, and he was too tired to keep walking, and he wasn't going to move from that spot until the next morning. When I realized that he was actually serious, I told him that he could do whatever he wanted, but I was getting out of there. In fact, I told him that when I got to the horses I would be taking both of them with me. I would come back in the morning and pick him up then. I went on to explain that staying here made about as much sense as spending the night in a walk-in freezer at zero degrees or even below. I felt that at least one, if not both of us, would have frostbite before morning, and if he wanted to stay, he would be doing it alone. I stood up and asked if he was coming with me. He grudgingly got up and followed me back to the horses. Then on the way out he started complaining about his horse, and said he wanted mine, so I traded him horses and he still complained.

The next morning as I was saddling up the horses, he said he didn't care how big that old tom lion was, he was not going back in there. Now he wanted to hunt somewhere else. Well, I asked him, just where do you want to do this? He didn't know where, but he wasn't going back there. Okay with me I said, we'll hunt on the west side of the river, north of Johnsondale, because right now I didn't feel that he was deserving of that particular lion anyway. Here's a guy that hired me to catch him a lion of any size and this was a no-catch no-pay type of hunt. Meaning that if he went home empty-handed, his hunt was free. The lion that I let go the week before would definitely set a record in the Boone and Crocket record book, and now he didn't care about size. So, to satisfy him, we left to hunt on the west side of the river, between Johnsondale and the Needles Peak. That area did have lion activity in it, though not as frequented by lions as often as the east side, but it was worth a try. We went over there and scouted it out but had no success. There was very little sign of any deer and if any lions were there, they would most likely only be passing through. On the third day, Don, a friend of mine from the Posey area, showed up to help with the hunt. He was quite the character, was tougher than nails, had no quit in him, would do anything needed to help, and by then, I needed some humor.

The three of us headed back to the same place on the west side of the river and just below the Needles Peak, with only two horses. My client/hunter stayed on horseback all the time, while Don and I shared my horse. This was something Don and I would do when there was only one horse between the two of us. The rule was, one of us would ride for an hour while the other walked and then we would trade. We rode all day looking for any sign of a lion, and had no luck. It just didn't look like there was much of any activity going on there, but what else would we do? Then on the morning of the fourth day, as we were starting to head back to hunt the west side again, this guy starts telling me that he now wants to go back to the Rincon Trail and hunt for the big old lion. In fact, he was insisting that we do as he requested, but as I said before, at that point I didn't think he was deserving of that lion, or any lion, for that matter. Hunting that trail was a long haul in and back out again and with having only two horses someone would again have to walk half of it. From what I had seen the day before, I doubted that this guy would volunteer to do anything like that. Don was game, but I wasn't, and I told him we were heading back for one more try on the west side and if that didn't work we would go back to the Rincon Trail on the following day, and that would be his last day of the hunt.

We loaded up and headed north out of Johnsondale, on the road that went under the Needles Peak, and just for fun I let my dogs out to hunt on the road. We were on the east side of Sentinel Peak, close to Carver Camp, and the dogs had hunted the road for about a mile and just before we reached the crossing of Alder Creek, they struck the trail of something that had recently been there. It was a hot trail and at first I thought it might be a bobcat, but after looking around I saw where a lion had been there, and not long ago. They hadn't gone far when they turned west and went up the north slope of Sentinel Peak. After about a mile run they treed a male lion that was average to a little above average in size.

The client did all right climbing up the mountain with us and made a clean one shot kill. Then Don and I (mostly Don) carried the lion down the mountain and back to the truck. We stopped several times to catch our breath, took some photos, and had an all around good time. This guy was thrilled with what he had done, Don was having a good time as well, and I was just happy it was over with. So, we're done. Or were we?

Don had a hair-lip, and was well known for bar room fights and his loud mouth, which some thought to be amusing while others didn't. By now Don had the ripeness of a man who rarely showered. At this point, he was a total mess and looked like he had just been in a street fight. He had his own vehicle with him, so he didn't need a ride back home, so he left about five minutes ahead of us. He told us to meet him at a local bar in Kernville. That sounded good, and I thought we could all use a drink right about then. This place was one of the nicest bars in Kernville at the time. It had a U-shaped bar so that when you entered, you approached at the bottom of the U as each side of it went toward the back, with the bartender in the middle. The windows were all covered with thin curtains and the lights were typically dim, with just enough light to where you could see everyone. I had been there several times before and it seemed that most of the regular customers usually sat up toward the front, close to the entrance.

When we got there, we noticed that Don was standing alone and leaning against the center of the U, with two mugs of beer on the bar in front of him. He was drinking from the one in his right hand as he held onto the other full beer with his left. There were about ten people sitting on stools to our left, all the way towards the end, and as far away from Don as they could get. The bartender, Art, who I was familiar with, was standing close to the others, also keeping his distance from Don. Thinking nothing of this, we went straight over to him and he greeted us with his usual hearty hello, hollered at the bartender to bring two more glasses and a pitcher of beer for the two of us, and said he was buying. It was easy to see that everyone in there was paying attention and Art wasted no time in doing as he asked. Then Art motioned for me to go with him, Art had some questions.

The two of us walked over to a quiet corner, about twenty feet from everyone, where we could talk in private. Then, very quietly, he asked if I knew this guy, what happened to him, and if he was safe. He went on to say that when Don first came through the door, he walked straight up to the bar and ordered a beer, and before Art could get the first drink to him he ordered another one. Art said he sucked down the first one as fast as he could, started on the next one, then ordered another. Keep in mind that Don had not cleaned up since he first arrived at my camp three days earlier, and he was still covered with dirt and dried blood from the lion, with sticks and leaves still hanging out of his hair and he smelled like an old billy goat. Art said they all thought this guy must have just killed someone outside the bar, and although they were all afraid of him, Art was even more afraid to not serve him. The telephone was too far away for anyone to get to it without him seeing them, so they simply decided it would be best to stay put until someone could come to their rescue before he could get drunk and go as crazy as he looked to be. I told Art that he was a friend of mine and about what we had done just a few hours earlier and assured him that everything would be okay, unless Don was provoked.

Eventually everyone calmed down, got a good laugh, drank a few more beers, then went outside to take a look at the dead lion and congratulated my client on his kill. From there we all headed for home, and the successful hunter went on his way with a load of memories and a lion hide. As for myself, I was happy, my dogs were happy, I had caught two lions in a little over a week, killed one, and that big old tom lion—he was still out there…

During the winter months that area was a natural for lions, very easy on the horses, and because of its lack of roads, it didn't have many other hunters coming into it. It was pretty good for what I was doing except for one thing: it was an in and out trail, which meant you could go in as far as you wanted, but when you were done, you had to turn around and cover the same ground coming out. So, a ten-mile hunt was really a twenty-mile ride. Despite this, I continued to hunt there, and from time to time it would pay off.

Don and his wife were the owners of a mountain resort not too far away from where I lived and they would close it down from the first of January until April 1. This gave Don the opportunity to join me if he had nothing else to do, plus he enjoyed the hunts and he was obviously a load of fun. Whenever we were in horse country, we always found ourselves with just one horse to share between the two of us. That was okay though, we were both able-bodied individuals who could walk, and we both enjoyed physical exercise, so we did what we always did and alternated with the horse. It didn't matter where we were riding, uphill, or downhill, one hour each was all we got.

By the middle of March, the weather had warmed up to where there wasn't any snow on the Rincon Trail, so I invited Don to go with me for a last run of the year. I went to the resort, picked him up and while he was packing his stuff into my truck, he informed me that he had only one pair of hiking boots and the left one was having repairs done on it in a shoe repair shop in Bakersfield. So, on this hunt he would be wearing his vibram sole hiking boot on his right foot and he had a slip-on type western boot with smooth soles for his left foot. Well, that was okay—it was *different*, but then again, so was Don.

We loaded up, went by my house to pick up my dogs, my horse, the camp trailer, and then we were on our way. The following morning we headed out looking for any lion signs, trading the horse as always. The ground was drying up and in most places we would be able to find the tracks if any lions had walked along or across the trail. It didn't look as though there were many deer in the area and no sign of any lions either. I wasn't surprised by this and figured that the warming weather could have pushed the deer to higher elevations, and into areas that were not an easy place to hunt. The terrain around there was steep, and there were few trails or roads. All this just reinforced my decision that this would be the last trip there for the season and I would move on.

As the two of us were going along the trail, there was one thing I noticed, Don was doing. It was my turn to ride my horse and Don was walking almost next to my horse, he was carrying one walking stick in each hand. With each step he would carefully place the point of one of those sticks into the ground, leaving a mark, it was like he was using them for a cane. He did this mile after mile. Finally, I asked him what he was up to and his answer was quite simple. He said, "If these tracks of ours stay here long enough, maybe the next people to come up this trail will see them, and think that there were two separate hikers going up the trail together. One missing his left leg, and the other was missing his right leg, and each having a peg leg. He did this for at least five miles. Was Don a little crazy? No, I don't think so, but then you never really know.

Don died in 1996 while hiking in the backcountry above Sonora, California. His ashes were then scattered by his son, Archie, in a place he loved to hunt, in the Southern Sierras of Tulare County. As for the old tom lion, I sure got a close look at him, but because the ground was frozen on that day, I was never able to see what his tracks looked like, all I saw was him and that was enough. I knew lion tracks, and had I seen any left by him, I would have known immediately who they belonged to. I never saw any signs of him again; it was like he had simply vanished. During the several years that I hunted in the area, the only other lions I caught there were females, which I found to be very interesting.

So the question is: was this the same lion that the State Lion Hunter, Howard Bilton, had talked about? If so, then there was no doubt that this area belonged to him. When I came along and caught him he must have been at least twelve to fourteen years old. There was also little doubt in my mind that my dogs and I were the only ones to have ever treed him, and I am the only person to have looked at him, eye to eye. It was at that time, I earned a new respect for lions in general and a total respect for him, a respect that he deserved. I also must admit, I'm actually glad that I never caught him again, and if he was killed by another hunter they would have let the entire country know about it, and that never happened. No, I believe that this old guy lived out his entire life in the Kern River drainage and ruled the same area where I caught him. I also suspect that he died there as well. Maybe another male lion killed him? Who knows? But then maybe he just curled up, went to sleep and never woke up again. We'll never know. I would like to think that he eventually died of old age, somewhere around the Rincon Trail.

Above is my friend Don Kinch helping out by packing a lion off Sentinel Peak. This type of terrain is typical to many parts of the Kern River Canyon.

Here I am crossing the Kern River at low water between Kernville and Johnsondale. During normal runoff all of these boulders are usually covered with swift rapids.

Looking at this photo doesn't look like much of a river, but don't be fooled. Crossing the Kern River even when the water level is low can be dangerous. During high levels it can be almost impossible to find safe places to cross. The bottom of this river is mostly boulders of all sizes, creating large holes between each of them large enough to swallow up a horse, rider, and all. A great area for the fishermen, but not so good if you slip and fall in trying to cross with horses. The Kern starts at and elevation of 13,600 feet, and in only 165 miles, it drops to 300 feet. It's a fast-moving river that has claimed over 300 lives in the past fifty years. I'm sure this is just one of the reasons country singer Merle Haggard wrote and sang the song "Kern River."

The Kern River Canyon
Looking towards the Kern Plateau.
Spot is in the foreground, I am on the right, along with our horse's.
No roads, and only game trails to get around. Still it made good lion country.
*Baker Point is directly behind the photographer,
and can be seen in the next photo.*

*Myself with Spot and Thunder at Baker Point in
Tulare County on a very hazy day.*

**Stormy Canyon, and Bull Run Basin is just to the right of us, and
the Kern River, which can barely be seen as a light colored ribbon
is in the far distance. It is a one mile drop in elevation, and almost
straight down from where we are standing before it starts to level out
at the river. When, or if the dogs drop off here, they have got their work
cut out for them, and so will anyone who tries to follow them.**

*As a pair of dogs, these two were both exceptional cold trailers, fast on the
track, hard hitting dogs, and it was almost certain that if they jumped it, it
was as good as caught. In the late spring of 1972, and within one month of
each other I lost both of them. Thunder died at the age of four from injuries
inflicted by a bear and Spot died from heartworm treatment. Saylor was
treated along with Spot, and they died within one day of each other from the
treatment. As a pair of dogs, Saylor and Spot were as powerful as any I had
ever hunted with. They were each in their prime of life at only seven years old.*

Chapter 10

TELEPHONE RIDGE

It was mid-August 1968 and as usual the hottest part of summer, with the daytime temperatures running above 100 degrees in the Glennville area, and not a drop of rain since mid-May, making it not only hot, but also extremely dry. I rarely had any hunters during that time of year. In order to keep my dogs in shape I would take them out during the night, turn them loose and see what they could come up with. Usually they would catch a raccoon, a bobcat, a bear, or an occasional lion. On this hunt it was during the late morning hours when I was hunting in the mountains above Glennville. I was on the Sandy Creek Fire road close to where it crossed Sandy Creek when my dogs treed a good size male lion. At the time, the lions in California were still classed as a predator, which gave them no protection of any kind, and because of this, anyone could do whatever they wanted with them. I had no hunters with me except for my friend Joe Bryan, who was along for the ride. Neither one of us had any intention of killing him, but at the same time, I really didn't want to let him go either. I knew that the lions were going to become a game animal, and before this happened I wanted to take one more lion alive, just for fun. So I decided to take him home alive. That way, when they made the lion a game animal, I could get a permit to keep him. Then I would have a live female and male lion in captivity.

I had a small female lion that I kept in a caged area in my garage, where I lived in Glennville. I was using her to train young dogs by turning her loose and letting them chase and tree her, then I would bring her back home, unharmed. She weighed only about sixty pounds, would run like crazy when I turned her loose, and as soon as the dogs caught up to her she would jump into a tree. I was careful to turn her loose where the trees were all small to medium sized oaks, which made it much easier to recapture her. She was perfect for the job, and a much easier choice than trying to do it with a larger lion.

As stated earlier, I owned a tranquilizer gun that I had purchased by special order at the local hardware store in Glennville. I had used it before with good results, but I was unable to get any of the prescription drugs that worked the best. So I was left with only some over-the-counter options that were available to anyone who owned livestock. It was risky stuff to use on lions, and although I wasn't completely happy with it, it did work, so I took what I could get.

The single most important thing was to get the dosage right. All the reports said that just a little too much could be fatal to cats. But one of the nicest things about the drug was that it was fast at knocking them down, so they couldn't get away from you. With that stuff, they couldn't get very far before passing out, which obviously made it easier to find them. On the other hand, the drug wore off fast, giving me only about fifteen to twenty minutes to get everything done. Before I could get started I needed to go back home and get the fifty-five gallon clamp-lid barrel I used to put them into after I had them on the ground. I left Joe with the dogs and the treed lion for about an hour while I went back home. We were also right along side the main dirt road so I would not be needing my horse to help pack him out.

The lion was treed about thirty feet up in a good-sized white fir tree that was about three feet in diameter at its base. Climbing up this tree to put a noose around his neck was out of the question, and since we were right next to the road it was about as good as it could get. So I broke out my tranquilizer gun. I guessed his weight at 135 pounds, and to be safe, I loaded the dart to about half the recommended dose and it hit him in the back leg. After the dart hit him, he immediately started moving around and backing down the tree, butt end first. All of this was happening at the same time and within a minute after he was hit, he paused at about fifteen feet up, then the drug hit him and he fell to the ground.

This tree was on a good downhill slope, which helped to soften his fall as he hit the hillside and then rolled almost into the road. Everything was working just right and in less than two minutes I had a noose around his neck. Then, I pulled him to a safe spot, stuffed him into my barrel, and within the next five minutes he was loaded into my truck, and we were heading for home. Sound easy? Well this one was, and just like that I was on my way.

It was only a 30 minute drive to my house, and by the time we got there the drug had worn off, and it was no doubt getting hot in that barrel, and I wanted to get him out A.S.A.P. I had a number of vent holes all over it that were about one and one half inches in diameter, but it was still summertime and I knew it was not very comfortable in there. As soon as I got home, I took the barrel with him in it to the cage, hooked it up to the cage so he could get out, and turned him loose into the cage with the female lion. The female lion was less than half his size. When he came out, he instantly charged her, bit off about six inches of her tail and the fight was on. What could I do? There was no way anyone could stop it. He was *pissed*. The fight lasted for only thirty to forty seconds, and had it lasted any longer he would have killed her for sure. Fortunately, for her he let go, and as soon as he did, she ran and hid.

The next thing he did was to start attacking the cage, which was made of the heaviest chain link I could find. He was pulling on the heavy gauge galvanized wire so hard that he was stretching it like it was made of aluminum. While he was doing this, I went and got my gun to shoot him just in case he got out or went back after the female lion. He pulled so hard on the wire fence that there were portions of it that were shaped like huge paper clips. This went on and off for the better part of an hour before he started to settle down. Did I say settled down? I should have said, slowed down, because he never gave up. After a couple of hours, I tried to calm him down by tossing in about ten pounds of frozen meat chunks, but he wasn't interested. All he wanted was to get out, and I knew that there had better not be anyone in his way if he did.

The cage where I kept these lions was at the back of a very old one-car garage at my house. It had a dirt floor, which was good for them, and I had covered the wooden sections of the back wall with sheets of thick aluminum sheathing to keep them from chewing a hole through the wood wall and getting out. The cage was about twelve feet long by eight feet deep and four feet tall. The front was covered with heavy-duty chain link fencing wire, as was the top. I also built a small day yard that I could open up to let them out into during the daytime. It measured, eight feet by eight feet, and about four feet tall. This was made of the same heavy chain link, and they could go back and forth as they wanted

After he started to settle down, I loaded up the tranquilizer gun again just in case he made another attack on the female, and then stuck around for a few hours to make sure that everything looked okay. Then I cleaned myself up and went to Austin's Café, which was only three doors away from where I lived, had a bite to eat, came back, fed the dogs, looked the lions over, and hit the sack. It was around eight the next morning when I went out to see how things were going in the lion cage, only to find out that sometime during the night that guy had torn the door off that went into the day yard, then he tore a hole into the outside fencing and they were both gone. I had no idea as to when they got out, and it was already getting hot outside. All of my dogs were so accustomed to having a live lion at home and living next to them that they hadn't made a sound; I guess they had just watched them leave. In fact, the lions had both walked within three feet of Liz's house, while she was still in it.

I immediately knew that I needed to try and get them back, and with the trailing conditions being very poor it was questionable if I could catch either one of them. I was surrounded by private property and not everyone wanted someone running hound dogs through their land, especially without permission. It was already hot and dry, and getting hotter by the minute, and I needed to act fast, and I needed some help. First thing I did was make a phone call to Roy Stephenson and told him what was going on and he said he was on his way. Together we started trailing them in the dusty dirt around the house, found that they had gone, side by side down my neighbor's driveway to the west, then turned towards the GMVA Rodeo Grounds. They were still together when they arrived there. These two walked side-by-side, straight across the rodeo ground arena, entering at the north west corner and left on the east side, just where the bronc riding stalls are at.

Next, they crossed Angel Creek and went between two houses and then back up into the hills where I first found them. By the time I got the dogs after them it was getting so hot that there just wasn't enough scent left to trail. I lost them both and they were never to be seen by anyone again. As one could imagine, it took only hours for word to spread all over that small ranching community that Ed Vance had just let two mountain lions escape, and they all knew that I lived right in the middle of town. As one might imagine, some people were furious, while others didn't seem to care at all, and then there were those who thought it was actually funny.

I had to admit that I was one of the amused ones, but this made it three lions that had escaped from me at that same location. The first was a very young male that was only days old when I first got him, that had opened his eyes probably not long before I captured him; I had no idea what had happened to his mother. This little guy was not vicious, but he wasn't that easy to handle either. I had always heard that if you can catch them before their eyes are open, they don't know anything about their mother yet and will usually accept you, and this seemed to be the case with him. I kept him in my house for several months, had a litter box for him, fed him a milk formula for about a month, and from there on he had raw meat. I put a small collar on him and if I took him anywhere I would carry him in a burlap sack and wore welder's gloves, so I could handle him without losing any fingers.

I actually learned quite a bit from that little guy, such as the sounds the young ones actually make. Every night I would hear this little guy chirp like a bird as he walked through out the house. I had heard from other professional lion hunters that this was the way mountain lions communicate and sure enough, he was doing it. Of course they make other noises, the most common being hisses and growls. He had been living with me for about three months, when one day he got out through an unlocked screen door on the back porch. I had no idea how long he had been gone when I discovered this and no one in town saw anything of him either. He was just gone.

On several occasions, the local school would bring supervised field trips for the kids to see the lions. The kids really liked seeing them, and someone always wanted to see what would happen if something was stuck through the fence to where the lion could bite it, so I always tried to keep something available that I could sacrifice, usually a hard piece of a wooden broom handle worked well, or an oak limb that was about an inch or more in diameter. There was no need to poke the lions with anything, I just had to put it into the cage and instantly the stick would be snapped into pieces without any effort. The kids were always impressed and in its own way, it was educational as well.

These lions were definitely different from the ones that lived in a zoo all of their lives, and these kids could easily see that. Here was an animal that had been perfectly designed to kill and do it faster than you could blink an eye. The power in their jaws is unbelievable. So, if there was any lesson to be learned, it was not to put anything through that wire fence that you didn't want to lose. During the short period that I was doing this, I must say that I really enjoyed it. Plus there was a special satisfaction in being able to do this, especially when I would do it all by myself, and without the use of any drugs.

But the times were changing, and I suppose it was just as well that there were no more lions in my garage. Rumors were circulating about several powerful protection groups who wanted to change the status of the California lions. These groups took on the California Department of Fish and Game, claiming that there were less than six hundred lions left in the entire state, and they won the debate, without a fight; California Fish and Game must have been asleep or simply didn't care. I believed they were guilty of both. I put my lion catching equipment into storage and didn't use it again until I moved to Montana. At that time I had no idea that what I had been doing would simply become another part of western history.

When it came to feeding these lions, there was a local rancher by the name of Henry Bowen who supplied me with a large amount of meat from cows that had either died from natural causes, or were in the process of dying. Henry would always call me over to get it while it was still fresh and I could clean, cut it up, and then freeze it. On one occasion, Henry called me to come and get a bull that I think he killed, and when I got there, I was surprised to see how big this bull was. Calling this thing big was an understatement. It was huge. Henry told me where to find it. As usual, he told me to not worry about the guts, hide, head, etc. I can leave that, and have fun with the rest of it. It was just like he said, dead, but it hadn't been that way for long. I had never cut up an animal as large as this one before, but with a couple razor sharp knives, an axe, and a chainsaw, it didn't take all that long, and what I wanted was in the back of my truck. I cut it up into sections small enough for me to handle, and then I was on the road. From there I took it to Glennville and called Russ Carver on the phone. Russ was another old time rancher who's family roots went back to the early settlers, and he was all set up with a first class butcher shop at his ranch. At the time I only had a normal-sized chest type freezer that could only have held a quarter of the meat that was coming off this bull. As soon as I got back to my house, I called Russ to see if he was at home, which he was, and he told me to bring it on over. I could only imagine what went through Russ' mind when I drove into his place with a pickup truck full of dead beef. Right off he started asking me where I got it and what was wrong with this animal. As the two of us were loading it into his shop, I passed on all that I knew about it, which wasn't much. First thing he did was grab up a piece of the back, cut off a couple of rib eye steaks with his band saw that were about one and one half inches thick. He laid them on the counter and asked, are you sure that you want to give this to a mountain lion? Well, they did look pretty good, so I asked him. Tell me what you're thinking? He didn't have to think for long, He wanted to cut a deal; His offer was; in exchange for butchering this thing, he would take all of the prime cuts and the balance would be mine. Plus, he would keep in his freezer, all that I didn't have room for at home, and give it to me as I needed it. I didn't know just how much fresh meat I now had for both the lions and my dogs, but it was hundreds of pounds of pure meat. As we were going through all this, out of the corner of my eye, I noticed a young boy walking up to us. I had never seen him before, but it was easy to see that he was Russ' son. As I was being introduced to Nathan, Russ invited him into the butcher shop and told him what we were doing. Then the three of us unloaded all of the meat out of my truck and I was on my way. At the time Henry gave that bull to me, I had about six hounds and one adult male lion to feed, and it took over three months before they had eaten it all up. In fact, I had to decline other offers from Henry until this one was almost all gone. As years went by, Nathan eventually came to run this cattle ranch in the same way his father did.

1968

This was the last lion that I took alive while in California

Lightly sedated with just enough tranquilizer to calm him down. (I had never tried using both a half dose of tranquilizer and ropes before), but it worked pretty good.

Notice, there is no pole between the two of us, just a cable and noose.

This was easy. Just thread the cable through the bottom of my 55 gallon barrel, pull him in, and clamp on the lid. Got him.

This is me with the male lion that tore up the cage in Glennville. At the time he was a little loopy from the drug that I had given him only a few minutes earlier, and after seeing the way he acted when he was caged, it's definitely a good thing he was drugged here. As you can see, there was no pole between us, just a quarter inch cable. Within a few minutes of this photo he was in a barrel and we were headed down the road.

Chapter 11

CHANGING LANDSCAPE

While the world of hunting lions in all western states was being pressured to change by a number of protection groups, this was especially the case in California, where they seemed to have a better hold on the politicians and lobbyists were welcomed. In many ways, I could see why the groups felt the way they did, especially if they were privy to the same reports or stories that I was. There were only a few hound hunters who were considered outlaws, and they were definitely giving the rest of us a bad name. There was nothing anyone could do to stop them, and many respectable hunters feared that soon all hound hunting would be finished, and it didn't appear that there were many state game wardens who cared enough to do anything about it either.

So in June of 1969, I found myself writing letters to the California Department of Fish and Game and to Ronald Reagan, the Governor of California. I wrote with the hope that we who followed the rules would never lose the right to hunt with hounds, and to speak out against the indiscriminate killing of bears. Much to my surprise, I actually received responses from the Director, G. Ray Arnett, and an assistant to Reagan, but as I sort of expected, they both said they didn't have enough money to do any more than they were already doing. In other words, nothing could be done to stop what was coming.

Around that same time, I got a phone call from the local game warden around Glennville, asking for my help in relocating a bear that was tearing up a cabin in Sugarloaf Mountain Park. He said that he would also be bringing the head game biologist for Fish and Game in Sacramento, and we could all meet in the morning at the Sugarloaf Lodge, which was about a mile from the cabin. He went on to say that they would need to use my tranquilizer gun since they didn't have one with them. I was fine with this, but when I met up with them, I was surprised to see that they were driving a passenger car. It didn't seem right, but I was going to go along with it, just to see how they did things. I followed them up the mountain to the cabin and sure enough, there had certainly been a bear in that cabin. To get in, it had broken out a window in the front door, completely trashed the inside, refrigerator, cabinets, furniture, and all. Then it broke out a window on a far wall and made its exit. I think it may have still been there when we drove in, because the trail was so fresh. When I turned the dogs loose, they tore off running as fast as they could and within a half mile, the bear was up a tree, and just a short distance from a road.

Since we were traveling in separate vehicles and everything happened so fast at the cabin, I hadn't had any time to ask how they were going to pull this off. When we got to the tree, the head biologist acted like he was more concerned about getting the bear captured than doing any talking, so I just stood back and watched. He asked for my tranquilizer kit, which held a number of syringe darts that held doses of one to five cc's. The bear was an adult female that I guessed her weighed, maybe 125 pounds at the most. I had never tranquilized a bear, but I did know something about my equipment, including how much to use. I thought that one and a half cc's would be adequate for a bear of that size, but that's not what they were thinking. The biologist wanted to hit it with five cc's, so he grabbed the five cc dart and filled it to the top. I felt this would kill the bear, and I told him as much. But he didn't care; he acted like he hadn't heard a word that I said.

So I told him again. He cut me off and said he had transported many live bears before, and he knew what he was doing. By then, I was beginning to think one of two things: either he had no idea what he was doing, or more likely, he knew *exactly* what he was doing. Either way, there was no doubt in my mind what was about to happen, I just didn't know why.

He darted the bear and as soon as the drug started to take effect it bailed out of the tree and ran off. I didn't think it would go far with that much of the drug in it, so I left all of my dogs tied up with the wardens while I put Saylor on a leash. The two of us followed it through the woods and found it about two hundred feet away. I tied Saylor to a tree, and went back, got the rest of my dogs and the two of them, and took them to the bear. Once we got set up with the downed bear, the biologist put a piece of oak in its mouth and secured it in place around its head with bailing wire, which is the same technique I used to keep live lions from biting while tying them up. While this guy continued tying up her feet, I noticed that the bear was no longer breathing. I told the biologist this twice before he would pay any attention to what I was saying. What I was saying was the bear is not breathing, and then he started pushing on its ribs like he was trying to get its heart going. He put on quite a show and he even acted as if he was really concerned. Then I told him that he wasn't getting anywhere and perhaps he should try a little mouth-to-mouth resuscitation. By now I was totally disgusted with both of them and wasn't buying any of it. I then told them that if they had just wanted to kill the bear they should have simply shot it.

This biologist continued to act like he was sorry. By then I had had enough and I wanted the truth. "Okay," I said. "Let's come clean. You came here in a four door passenger car with only a small roll of bailing wire and you think I'm going to buy your story about live transporting this bear to another location! Someplace where it would not cause anyone any trouble?" I continued telling them that if they were so stupid to try something like that, and should the bear regained consciousness before they got to their destination, she would tear this car and both of them up getting out.

I repeated, I wasn't buying their story and if they didn't start telling me something I could believe, then my next stop would be the newspaper in Bakersfield and maybe they would like to explain it to them.

They finally got the message and started talking. First it was the warden, who told the biologist that they needed to start being honest with me. They said that because of legal liabilities, they couldn't relocate problem bears in California, and that included all national parks within the State. Most of the problem bears were caught in traps specially designed for the job, called culvert traps. When the bear went in and pulled on the bait, the door dropped down and locked it in. From there it was driven away to where no one else would be watching when it was simply shot and killed while it was still in the trap. They went on to say that there were many dumping sites where they could just back up their vehicles and push the dead bears out of the trap and off a cliff—problem solved.

So I asked them, why all this? What was this all about? They went on to explain that Fish and Game was trying to improve its image with the general public, and they thought that by fooling me into thinking that they actually did relocate a problem bear, I would advertise what a good job they were doing, and this would help to take some of the pressures off in the area. The biologist said he expected the bear would die from an overdose of the drug, but not so soon. In other words, he thought it would live long enough for them to stuff it into their trunk, and I would never know the difference. It was a fiasco, but it was their show, and after all they were the "professionals."

Not long after this, I received a phone call from a friend who lived in Porterville and worked part time for the U.S. Forest Service. He told me that he had just came out of their morning briefing and the subject for the day was, going after *me*. He went on to say, there was a group of about six men who were on their way to Glennville, hoping to find me, and their mission was to stop me from guiding on National Forest land. He didn't understand what their reasoning was, but he wanted me to be ready. It was about nine in the morning when he called, and Porterville was about an hour drive, so I did my morning chores and then walked over to the gas station, where I thought I might run into them. Sure enough, there they were, about half a dozen of them just as I was told.

The leader was a real big guy. He told someone at the café they were looking for me, and after someone pointed me out, he walked over and introduced himself. Then he immediately started telling me that I could no longer guide in the National Forest without first obtaining a special use permit. If I were caught doing this without "all these permits," I would be cited, fined, and maybe even arrested; he was basically telling me to *Keep Out*.

I had never heard of such a thing, and started asking some simple questions, like, how much does one of these permits cost? Why would I need a permit since I don't set up camp in the National Forest? And why were they here in the Greenhorn district when their area was actually the Hot Springs district? He said it didn't make any difference where he was from, it was all government land and because I was making money while I was in the National Forest, I would need a permit. The longer we discussed this the more it became apparent that he was only following orders and really didn't know what he was doing. He then instructed me to call the Forest Service district ranger at California Hot Springs, and he would tell me what I needed to do. I knew the guy, so I called him.

Our conversation lasted for about three minutes. He said I would need separate permits to do what I was doing for each Forest Service district where I hunted—about fifteen districts, throughout the state. He would be the one handling all of the permits, regardless of where they were, and the cost for each was around one hundred dollars per year. I told him that I had never heard of anyone being required to do this. I knew others who did the same thing I was doing and as far as anyone knew: all that was needed was a State guide license, which I had. Then I hung up. It wasn't but a day or two later when my friend in Porterville called again and told me that the order was now out to all forest rangers to get Ed Vance for anything they could drum up on me. It was hard to believe this was happening.

So I called my friend John McNally, the Tulare County Deputy Sheriff, in the Kernville area, who was also a licensed guide and backcountry packer. John had dealt with the U.S. Forest Service for many years and probably knew their operations better than most of their employees. I explained my situation and he told me to go over to the Hot Springs headquarters and tell them that I was now working for him, and if they had any problems with me, to give him a call. So, I rounded up my friend Don Kinch, and the two of us went to see the Hot Springs Supervisor.

As always, Bruce greeted us with a smile and a handshake, then asked what the visit was about. I wasted no time getting right to the point: Why are you after me? He was at a loss for words at first, and then he brought up the permits. We had discussed this for about sixty seconds when I told him that John McNally was now my boss and if he had any complaints he should take them up with him. Our meeting was over almost as soon as it had started, and so was the issue about permits; he left me alone from then on.

The Forest Service seemed to be making changes in this part of the country at that time. I guess some of them just wanted to flex their muscles by pushing people around. Not all of their changes made much, if any sense; it was like they didn't want anyone using the forest. First I noticed they were putting up signs in campgrounds requiring all dogs to be tied up at all times, even if there is no one else using the camp and the range cattle were grazing between the tables leaving an ankle deep mess of manure.

They also started locking forest roads during certain months, or even permanently. In the beginning some very short and insignificant roads were closed down. I found some gates placed at the very end of some side roads, and then after a couple years, they started moving those same gates closer to the main entrances off the main roads. This stopped all vehicle traffic, except for theirs. When asked why they were doing this they claimed they couldn't afford to maintain the roads and needed to cut down on erosion, which happened regardless. And of course, their vehicles didn't cause any erosion or if they did, they could justify it. All of these new regulations would apply to everyone but them.

Many times I would be walking or riding my horse inside the locked gate and Forest Service vehicles or even a caravan of their vehicles, would drive past me. More than once I would find a bunch of Forest Service personnel sitting in trucks or buses, behind a locked gate and doing nothing. One day as I was riding my horse on the Sandy Creek Fire Road, I stopped one such group and asked why they were driving there when it was closed. The driver paused only long enough to say they always used it as a shortcut, and quickly drove away. So, why all these changes? That part of Sequoia National Forest was not a heavy-use area, and in fact, during the months that these roads ended up being locked, I could go for weeks on end without seeing anyone else. And when it came to maintenance the Forest Service would run a road grader across most of these roads once every three years and that was it. If a tree fell across a road in the mean time, and you wanted to go through, then it was up to you to clear it.

At this same time the Forest Service brought in a new forestry graduate to run the Fulton Ranger Station above Glennville. He grew up in New York State, and received his credentials from a college there, and then the Forest Service hired him. According to him, he was sent to Glennville to "straighten things out." He went right to work and it didn't take him long before he became the most unpopular ranger ever to have lived in the area. For myself, I got along with him to a point, and I even took him on hunts and eventually he killed a lion with me.

It was obvious that Art wanted to make a name for himself, so he started researching old nearby mining claims and discovered that most had not been used since the end of World War II. Some of them had buildings on Forest Service land, but their special use permits had expired due to lack of use. The mines were abandoned because the price of carbide was too low to cover the cost of mining, so Art sent letters advising the prospectors to remove the buildings. He gave them only so many days to do so, and the day after the deadline had passed, he would load up some of his rangers and they'd go and blow these places up with dynamite. One right after another. He loved doing this and bragged to everyone about it. He went so far as to blow up an old, hand-hewn log structure that was originally used by the early settlers, and it could have been there before the road across Greenhorn Summit was built. I was sure that if it had been left alone it would have eventually been designated a place of historical significance. Art kept going until he blew up a cabin in the Piute Mountains, which ended up starting a fire. This one got him into trouble. After blowing it up, he and his crew left a little too early, and while driving down the road he heard a call come in from the lookout at Tobias. The person in the lookout was looking at smoke coming from the cabin he had just blown up. Art panicked, and called in for air support, and turned around and headed back, only to find that there was no need for the airplanes that were already headed his way. That did it! Art had caused enough trouble in the Greenhorn District. So what happened to Art? He was moved to another location, and with a promotion.

It seemed like everywhere I looked, big changes were being made, changes only appreciated by those who were setting them in motion. I felt that most of the people who were moving into those mountains did so because they liked what was there and wanted to become part of that type of living. So, why change anything? Unfortunately, there were those who liked change, especially when they are in charge. Not me, I liked things being the way they were so well that I wanted it to become a part of my life. I didn't want to change anything. I liked it the way it was, but if I could have changed anything, I would have gone backwards about one hundred years

At the time I had no idea of what was coming, I couldn't yet see the big picture. It's only now that I can look back and see that when I first started hunting, I was actually at the beginning of the end of an era. The old-time way of hunting and people's views on country living were changing. Like it or not, it was coming. The old lion hunters that once roamed these hills, hunters like Jay Bruce, Charlie Ledshaw, Howard Bilton, and others that few knew were there, are now gone. All that's left of this, is knowing there was a time when they were here, and at that time there was only one way to get it done, and that was the hard way. Today they are only a part of history, a history that unfortunately cannot be duplicated.

Though I wished that I could have lived a hundred years earlier, maybe I wouldn't have liked it as much as I thought I would, but it sure sounded good to me. I loved hearing about the stories of old times, and I would never pass up the opportunity to learn more about those years. For instance, there was a neighbor of mine who lived next door to me for only about a year before he died. Ben Youngman was his name. He died in 1970 at the age of around ninety, and I always thought it interesting that he was born around 1880. He always seemed to have a cigar in his mouth and he was a fine old gentleman. I really enjoyed visiting with him and he loved telling me about times when he was growing up in the foothills of Glennville. He said there were no real roads, just dirt trails. If you wanted to go somewhere, he said, you had to walk. Or you could ride a horse if you had one, or maybe have it pull a buggy or wagon.

He said he could remember when there were no barbed wire fences and you could ride any direction that you wanted without getting into trouble. That was unless you ran into some outlaws. He would talk about people knowing where their food came from, and so on, and unemployment meant you needed to find a job, and if you didn't work, you probably wouldn't eat either. It took days to get to the valley and back. Stories like that meant a lot to me. It sounded like a simpler way of life, but I was sure it was a harder way of life as well. I felt that most of the people in those mountains were there because they belonged there, and they wanted to get along with each other.

But, I was having to deal with people who had other ideas. People who enjoyed being in control of others, whether their decisions were right or wrong, and thought it was funny to go around blowing up buildings for no reason. Or trying to fool the locals into believing they were doing their job when they were in fact, deceiving the same public that was paying their wages. Making decisions on how to manage animals that they knew little or nothing about, or even trying to run some hunting guide out of business, just because they could, while at the same time getting paid to do all this crazy stuff.

These things started to bug me, but I could see there wasn't anything I could do about it. After Art was transferred from the Greenhorn District to a station up next to the Oregon border and promoted, he eventually received too many complaints there and Art was transferred to another station at Bishop. In my hunting travels I would stop by and visited with him on occasion and much to my surprise he admitted to me that he had made some terrible mistakes when he was in Glennville, and that was the reason why they moved him out. To him, he regretted blowing up the cabins that belonged to so many other people, and the worst of all was the old log building on Cedar Creek. I was pleased to know that Art had a change of heart, but the damage was done.

Chapter 12

NORTHERN CALIFORNIA

IN 1967 THROUGH 1968, THE BEAR POPULATION IN THE SOUTHERN SIERRAS WAS NOT GOOD ENOUGH FOR ME TO EXPECT THAT I COULD HAVE A HIGH RATE OF SUCCESS IF I TRIED HUNTING THERE THE ENTIRE SEASON. So I made plans to go north to Shasta County and hunt there until the heavy rains started by mid-November, then I would return home and finish out my hunts in the Greenhorn Mountain area. Some of the older hunters in that part of the Sierras told me that during the late 1950's there had been a very severe drought that greatly impacted the local bear population. At that time 1080 poison was widely used to kill ground squirrels, and I could only imagine how many bears had come along and ate their carcasses to have only been killed by the poison, the same stuff that killed my dogs, Pat and Rebel. What I can say for sure is that there were not many bears in that area until around 1969, and then the population began to increase. By 1972, I was able to stay there and hunt throughout the entire season and still expect a success rate of close to a hundred percent.

Liz was a tough little gal. Jim picked her up at an animal shelter in Susanville, California, when she was about one and one half years old. I guess someone didn't care for her, and took her to the pound just to get rid of her. All I can say about that is, if they were a bear hunter, they had no idea of what they were throwing away. I saw more than one bear take Liz down, and get on top of her, and as soon as she could get out from under it, she was right back after it again. I never saw her with any serious injuries

The 1967 season in Shasta started out like gangbusters. I had four dogs by then: Bo, Saylor, Bo's son Thunder, and Liz. They were in the best of shape, the weather was cooperating, and we were catching a bear almost every day that we hunted, including some very large ones, which made my hunters happy. My friend, Jim Bridges, who lived at Montgomery Creek, wanted to join in on some of my guided hunts and I welcomed him to come along. He knew the areas very well, had excellent bear dogs, and I felt for the first time I might have a friend to help with my bear hunts. The only problem with that was he worked in the woods Monday through Friday, and that left him with only weekends to hunt, or until they shut the logging down because of bad weather, and by then I would usually be gone.

The area was loaded with bears and I had never seen so many of them anywhere else. It looked like there was an endless supply. The terrain was a mixture of everything from easy to extremely steep and rough, and when the rainy season set in it was a relentless rain. I would set up my camp on the Pit River close to the Pit #5 dam, which was a Pacific Gas and Electric (PG&E) campground, set up for their employees, mainly the big shots from places like San Francisco. The groundskeeper, who oversaw this campsite, was the dam keeper for the many dams in that area as well.

Roger and his wife lived right next to the camp. I had no idea who owned it when I first started camping there, and on my second day, Roger came over, introduced himself, and said that if I would keep everything cleaned up I could stay there. He and I eventually became good friends and I used the place as an ongoing base for the next four years. In between hunts, he would invite me up to his house and we would talk lions and bears and racecars. I had no interest in the cars, but Roger loved them, so he would also fill me in on some of that. He also kept the rainfall records for the area, and he told me that the average annual rainfall there was ninety-nine inches. I believed every word of that because there were times when I saw as much of a foot of hard rain hit the ground in just two weeks.

This was a typical hunting campsite for me. This one is on the Pit River, close to Big Bend, California. I camped here at the Pit #5 dam for 4 bear seasons. I never knew when I would be needing to move my camp to another location, and because of this I needed to be compact as I could get, and ready to go on a moments' notice.

As you can see I could load my horse into the back with the dog boxes on each side, hook up my trailer, and I was gone to another location. With this setup, moving could easily be done in less than one hour.

The closest place to get supplies was just down the road about five miles, at a place called Big Bend. It had a post office and a small store, plus an aboveground gas tank where I could fuel up. There was also a forty-acre Indian reservation and a grade school. Nearby, the Pit River emptied into Shasta Lake and there were tens of thousands of acres of prime bear hunting. Also, in years past Del Norte, Humboldt, Trinity, and Siskiyou Counties had accounted for about thirty percent of all the bounties for lions throughout the entire state. But those high bounty years seemed to be gone, as those counties weren't producing lions like they used to, and anyway, there were so many bears that I couldn't see how I could ever keep my dogs on any lion before they were off chasing the fresher scent of a bear. The only way I could hunt for lions was when the bears were denned up in the winter, and that was when it was raining way too much for me. So that's when I returned to my home base of Glennville, and for the first time since I had started guiding hunts, I didn't need to find outside jobs to make ends meet; I was *busy*.

Bo would be turning ten years old in the spring of 1968, and he was starting to show his age. The gray hair all over his face was proof that he was getting too old to hunt the way he had in the past. In the years that he was with me, he had hunted in many parts of California, Utah, Nevada, Oklahoma, Arkansas, Missouri, and even in the swamps of Mississippi and Alabama. Everywhere he was put on the ground he did an outstanding job. During those few years he had caught or helped to catch over forty lions, well over a hundred bears, hundreds of bobcats, foxes, and who knows how many raccoons. He was a mentor for all my younger dogs at that time and for me as well. But now he had grown old, and was having trouble competing with the younger dogs, the same ones that learned so much from him. Yet even at ten, he wasn't completely washed up as a hunting dog, so in early 1969, just as he was turning eleven, I thought it would be best to find him a new home. He was too old for me to put with these younger dogs anymore, and living alone, I had no one to take care of him when I was gone. It was easy to see he could still be used effectively as a lion dog, especially if someone needed a well-trained dog to help train the young ones.

I knew a guy who lived just west of Bakersfield who had been on a few lion catches with me; he loved to lion hunt, but was never able to get any dogs of his own that could do the job for him. He did most of his hunting in the Los Padres National Forest, of Ventura and Santa Barbara counties, which had a fair amount of lions. It was not the easiest place to catch them, but they were there. Of all the places that I had hunted, it was by far the most difficult for both man and dog. It was all bare ground trailing and most of the time it was very dry and usually hot, with very few roads or none at all, so it was done in the old traditional way: You walked as you looked to find tracks in the dry dirt, and if you left the trail, you were either on your hands and knees or plowing through hard, interwoven, chaparral and Manzanita brush that was usually over your head.

None of this made it easy, but it was where he liked to hunt, and Bo always did well there, so I thought it might be a good place for him to live out his years. He was good to his dogs and I thought, if he wanted Bo, then I was willing to let him take him. I made the offer and before I knew it, Bo was gone. But he was in good hands, and it wasn't long before Bo had caught this guy his first lion, so everyone was happy.

While going over Bo's qualities, I feel it would only be right to mention his faults as well. In his old age, his obsession with food was out of control. Any type of food would take precedence over everything and to an extreme. More than once, I was out hunting and he would go missing and I would find him in a public campground where he tipped over trash barrels and scattered garbage all over the place. Even worse, he would help himself to campers' groceries while they looked on in complete despair, and not knowing what to do. He hadn't always been like this, but when he turned nine it became a problem.

I will always remember one time while I was camped at the Pit #5 campsite on the Pit River and I had to make a run into Redding, which took about four hours, round trip. When I got back into camp, I noticed that there were two men that had set up their tent and table about a hundred feet from my camp. Though all the other dogs were still hooked up, I saw that Bo wasn't on his chain and his stomach was so huge that it was all he could do just to stand up. One of the new campers walked over to me and asked if the dogs were mine, and when I said they were, he said that he, and his friend had arrived about three hours earlier, and after they set up their tent and were in the process of putting food on the table, Bo had somehow got off his chain, went over, and jumped up onto their table with all four feet. He began helping himself to everything edible that they had, including the packaging. He said Bo seemed to be friendly but they didn't think it was a good idea to step in and try to stop him. He was inhaling everything in sight and swallowing it down without chewing at all. They were stunned and impressed at the same time, and they just stood back and let him go at it.

They went on to say that within only a few minutes he had consumed two one pound T-Bone steaks, bone and all, a pound of liverwurst cheese and all their snacks, like cupcakes, donuts, chips, wrappers and all. Then they cut up a watermelon and offered him some and he even ate that, too. They were laughing the whole time as they told me this, but to me it wasn't funny at all. What could I do? I offered to pay for the damages, but they said that the show was worth more to them than all the food. Funny as it may have been to them, it came close to costing Bo his life; he couldn't eat anything for over a month. I ended up taking him to two different veterinarians; one in Redding and the other was in Porterville. They both gave him some medication, but nothing helped. They said that he must have injured his stomach lining by stretching it so much. The veterinarian in Porterville thought he was going to die of malnutrition, or more likely — starvation.. All I could do was take him home. After another day or so, I figured that he would die if he didn't get something into his stomach, and he needed fluid for sure. I tried cold and warm milk, then chicken broth, raw and cooked meat, but nothing interested him. I remembered reading in the Bible where it said to "take a little wine for your stomach's sake," so I went over to the Glennville Shopping Center which was only a few doors away. I didn't have much money, so I bought a bottle of the cheapest wine they had, "Red Mountain Burgundy." It only came in a one-gallon bottle. I let him smell it, then filled an eyedropper, squirted it into his mouth and for the first time in a long time, he swallowed something. I then stuck his nose into a small bowl of the stuff. Much to my surprise, he started drinking it up and after he finished what little was there, I added more to the bowl and he drank that too. I was amazed; he liked wine, and within three hours he was eating real food again. I only gave him small amounts for several days and then put him back on his regular feedings. It took only about a week before I noticed he was gaining weight, and within another two weeks, he was back in the woods.

When Bo was young he was not hunted until he was a little over two years old, which was unusually old for most hunting dogs. According to J. D., he was a natural born hunter who was easily trained, never ran deer, coyotes, or any other off game; he was totally dedicated to running only raccoons, foxes and bobcats. In fact, he was such a dependable dog that I had a hard time convincing him to try catching lions or bears. There was no telling how many times in his life that he had crossed the trail of a catchable lion and just walked on by. But, that all changed once we had worked together and once he started to do it, he did it right. He was also exceptional at cold trailing, faster than most, and when he treed an animal, he had it. Throughout his life, the only bad habit I knew of was the one I just mentioned. I was informed that sometime after he turned 12 he was simply too old to be of much help any more. So he was retired.

1968

Myself with Bo, who was now almost eleven. Old age was closing in on him, and this would be the last winter that he would be with me. Old age had taken it's toll on him. In the five years I had him he taught me by example what good dogs were suppose to do. Perfect? No, not at all. Good? You bet he was. Actually, I'd say he was better than Good. On this day the temperatures were close to fifteen below zero.

Bo died in his sleep at the age of thirteen

Chapter 13

IRON CREEK

By the end of 1969 and with the help of John McNally, I was back to not worrying about the Forest Service coming after me or dreaming up ways to stop me from hunting on public land, and I was looking forward to the 1970 hunts. The lion was now designated as a game animal, which I actually supported. I had a group of highly skilled dogs, and there were plenty of bears to be hunted in Shasta County. I had some good groups of hunters already lined up, and there was one group in particular that I was looking forward to.

That summer I met some carpenters who were building a bunch of fancy houses on a recently purchased ranch just west of Glennville. The new owner, Jack Kent Cook, was well known in the professional world of sports. He kind of showed up out of nowhere and started buying up large ranches all around the area, one of which was once owned by the old radio comedy show stars, Fibber McGee and Molly. Story had it that Cook wanted to build a place in these mountains where he could bring some of his athletes to entertain them during their off season. I knew at the time he was the owner of the Los Angeles Lakers as well as the Forum auditorium where they played basketball. He started construction on all sorts of buildings, and the contractor and his crew were also from the L.A. area. The carpenters would stay there during the week, and spend their weekends back at home, or wherever they wanted to go.

One afternoon while I was at Austin's Café in Glennville, which was only a few doors from my house, I was introduced to these guys. Much to my surprise one of them was an avid bow and arrow hunter and on the advisory staff of Ben Pearson Archery, which I had never heard of. We hit it off and next thing I knew I was scheduling a bear hunt for him, George Wright, and his close friend Jim Dougherty. It wasn't long before George and his crew started staying at my house during the week while they were in town working, and unbeknown to me I had just made friends with two very well known archery hunters.

I had the two of them scheduled at the beginning of the next bear season, where they would meet me at my camp on the Pit River. I had already taken several bears in the weeks before they got there and in the process, Saylor had sustained some minor injuries and would be laid up for a couple weeks, so I had to use Spot as the main dog until Saylor recovered. I didn't raise or train Spot, but was lucky enough to talk my friend, Jim Bridges, out of letting me have him the year before. Besides being very fast, he also fought a bear up close, was as tough as nails, and had caught several hundred bears by then. The other dogs were Thunder and Bonnie, both Redticks and Bo's offspring, as well as Hammer, who was a Walker hound that I borrowed from my friend Louis Strawn.

It was easy to see that George and Jim were the best of friends, and it was agreed between them that if the first bear we caught was not what Jim wanted, but was still of trophy size, then George would take it. Conditions for bear hunting were about as good as it gets. The roads were dry and dusty, which made it easier to see tracks when looking for them in the roads. It was cool at night, which made trailing better for the dogs until midday, when it could become too hot. There were some big ones out there, that's for sure, but finding them at the right time was not always that easy to do. I only had five days for the hunt and I wanted these two to go home with at least one big bear.

The first day out, we headed for the upper portion of Iron Creek and Oak Mountain. We were sharing stories and since we were there, I mentioned that the previous season I had a couple of lazy hunters with me and one of them killed a huge brown colored black bear in that area. We had found its tracks on top of Oak Mountain and like most of the bears I've started up there, it went down into Iron Canyon and treed in the bottom. I told Jim and George that I was sure it could have been the largest bear that I had ever caught up to that time, and to this day I don't think it has been beat.

The hunter that killed it was somewhat overweight himself and he really didn't seem to care much about the hunt, all he wanted was to kill a bear. The dogs had treed it at the bottom of the canyon which was around a 1,500 foot drop in elevation from where we had to park my truck, and the hunter and his partner were not in great physical shape for what we were about to do. But we really didn't have any choices except go down to the dogs. We made our way down the mountainside, and after the big guy killed the bear, I told him and his friend that I'd be needing some help carrying the hide out and asked if they could pitch in.

Their answer was an abrupt no. In their opinion, I was hired to catch them each a bear, and do all the work they were simply there to do the shooting. I honestly believed that the hide alone was at least 125 pounds and I tried to explain that this bear was special and probably the largest bear I had ever caught. I wasn't asking them to do all the work, just give me a hand. As hard as it was to believe, they both were willing to just walk away and leave it right where it laid.. They didn't care; all they wanted now was to get out. I couldn't believe what I was hearing, but could see that they meant every word of it. I couldn't just walk off like that so I suggested that I could at least cape it out for the one who shot it and we leave the rest. They agreed, so I skinned it out from the head to shoulders only, and left the rest to rot in the woods. This was against all of my principles and had I known it was going to happen this way, I would never allowed this guy to shoot this truly magnificent animal. Then just before we started out the shooter wanted one of the bears front feet, so I cut one off for him. Then I loaded the hide onto my shoulders and started the climb out of the canyon.

When we were about three-quarters back to the road, the overweight shooter sat down and said he wanted a helicopter to be brought in to airlift him out. I noticed that he didn't have the bears foot, and asked where it was? He said he threw it away! Needless to say, I was getting a real dislike for both of these guys, and then I said that the likelihood of you getting a helicopter to come and get you, was slim to none, and even if one came, they would have to pay at least a couple of thousand dollars and they wouldn't get out until the next day. But, this big guy was dead serious and kept at this. Eventually I told them that if they wanted out, then they had to get up and start climbing, because I was leaving. That was all it took; they finally got up and walked out. Every once in a while I would get stuck guiding guys like that, however it was easy to see that nothing like this would happen with either one of these two..

We continued sharing stories with each other, mainly about hunting, and then somewhere along the way to Oak Mountain we found a decent-sized bear track that was fresh enough for the dogs to trail, and the race was on. As usual, the dogs bailed off into one of the deepest canyons in the area, faded out of hearing, and then were gone. We followed one of the many roads in the area, and about two hours later we could hear the hounds treed at the bottom of a canyon, about a mile away. When we got to the tree, George said he wanted to take it. With only one quick shot, he had his bear on the ground. We dressed it out and we were back at camp well before sunset.

Shasta County
Professional Bowhunter George Wright
with Pope & Young record book bear

The next day we found some fresh bear tracks, but nothing like we were hoping for, so we passed up on all of them. The following day I thought we should try an area known as the Flat Woods. I had never had much luck hunting there, but thought it would be worth a try. We made it there early in the morning, but found nothing at all. The roads were all very dusty and if a bear crossed any of them it would be easy to see their tracks, but nothing. It looked like the day was going to get pretty warm and if we were to have any luck catching a bear, we needed to get something going before it got too late. I just wasn't sure where to go. With a little process of elimination, I realized that I hadn't been up to Chalk Mountain for quite a while, so I drove us back toward where we were camped, crossed the Pit River at the Pit #5 Powerhouse and we headed up the river as fast as I dared go.

As soon as we hit the Chalk Mountain dirt road, one of them asked where we were going. I could tell they were wondering what was on my mind, since I hadn't said a word since we left the Flat Woods about thirty minutes earlier, but I was trying to figure out where our bear was. All I could say was that I wasn't sure just yet; I just had a feeling that I needed to keep going in that direction. Then, there they were: the fresh tracks of a very large bear. It had come down from Chalk Mountain, walked straight down the road toward us and then it turned to the west and dropped over the side of the road and into the canyon below. As soon as I stopped the truck to take a better look, they both asked me what I saw at the same time, and my answer was exactly what they wanted to hear. We've got a keeper!

We all got out and it was easy to see that it was for sure a big one. I got Spot out to see how he would react, and as expected, he was ready to go; it was a smoking hot track, and probably not that far away. So I dropped the tailgate of my truck and put the whole bunch after him, all at the same time. They all left out with their heads in the air, and went only about a quarter mile before they caught up to him, and then the race was on. He was traveling west, parallel to the river and about a mile above it. In the beginning we were so close to camp that we could hear Saylor back there barking, wishing he could come along. We left the truck parked where we turned them loose and followed on foot. Once the dogs caught up to the bear, he ran only a short distance before he had decided he had enough of them and turned to fight.

For a while, they were almost out of hearing and it looked like it was trying to go back in the direction where he had come from, except the dogs were putting on the pressure so hard that he kept on a steady walk to the west. They were doing a good job of holding him at bay, which helped us to catch up. The closer we got, the easier it was to tell that there was a pretty good fight going on. Both Spot and Thunder were the kind of bear dogs that would get in real close and clamp on when the opportunity came up. Spot almost always would be looking straight into its face from only a few feet away, while Thunder grabbed a mouthful of hide from behind. This method usually worked well on the tough ones, and that's what was happening when we showed up.

It usually doesn't take a whole lot of that type of pounding before most bears look for a tree, and just like so many others, he went up a hundred and fifty foot Ponderosa Pine. He made it halfway up and stopped on two large limbs. Where he was at, we could see that this was not going to be an easy shot, especially with an arrow. The only place we could find that was clear enough for Jim to make his shot was up the hillside, which would put him higher up, and the shot would be a long one of about a hundred and fifty to two hundred feet. He'd also have to shoot past some large branches and limbs, which left no room for error.

As Jim got into position, George was busy readying with his sixteen-millimeter movie camera so he could film the action. I was hoping he could make the shot and that it would be a fast, clean kill. From where I was, it was interesting to watch as Jim released the first arrow and see how it bent from front to back as it left the bow. The thrust of the bow pushing against the back of the arrow made the arrow bend from front to back and then it would create a slight but straight wobble all the way to the target, which in this case was the bear. Because of the long distance between the two of them, it made these bends three times before hitting the bear in his rib.

That was an impressive shot, and one that not everyone could pull off. But then just as fast as this arrow hit it, it bounced back off his side and then fell to the ground. As soon as that happened the bear started sliding down the tree so fast that it was almost like he was in a free fall, ripping off tree bark and small limbs all the way down. When it was about half way down, Jim cut loose with another arrow hitting him again. This time it stuck deep into his shoulder area. It was easy to see that Jim is deadly with his bow, and it took only a few seconds from the time he was hit with the first arrow until he hit the ground, and along with him came a large cloud of tree bark, limbs, pine needles, and dust. This was quite a sight to be watching, but right now, I have a very large and wounded bear that is back onto the ground and all four of my dogs are grabbing ahold of him and the fight was on again. Within seconds, the dogs and bear had disappeared into the heavy brush and were heading downhill.

What was happening now had caught all of us by surprise, and there were few choices, accept to stay with the dogs, so here we go again. It was doubtful that this bear would be looking for another tree. Instead, he was on the fight and to stop him, someone would have to kill him on the ground.

As soon as we caught up to them, Jim shot the bear four more times, and he did it almost as fast as I could have done with my lever action rifle. Again, one right after another the arrows kept breaking apart at the tips upon contact. None of us had ever seen anything like this, and to say that the bear was pissed off would have been an understatement. He was charging in every direction with the dogs all over him and it was getting uglier by the second. The dogs seemed to have thrown all good sense to the wind and were attacking the bear as if he wasn't fighting back and couldn't hurt them, which wasn't the case at all. While they had him surrounded and jumping all over him, he was trying to run everyone of them down. At one point, he turned and would have gotten Jim down into the dirt had it not been for the four dogs all over him. Then, with Spot baying in the bears face, the bear ran Spot down, forcing him to the ground, and completely smothered him with his huge body, to the point we couldn't see any part of Spot. Almost as fast as he took Spot down, Spot came rolling out from under him, but with some deep wounds to his leg.

Meanwhile, the other three dogs were all over the bear, with two of them even on top of his back. The entire situation had gone out of control and was a wild and crazy brawl. The bear was large enough that the dogs couldn't hurt him and at the same time he had the size and ability to kill every one of them and any of us as well. When it came to weapons, all that we had between us was Jim's archer setup and my sawed off .30-.30 Winchester rifle. George was armed only with his camera equipment, which he wasn't using because he and I were busy trying to collect any arrows that had bounced off of the bear and get them back to Jim.

We were now about two miles from where it all started, and it didn't look as though any of the arrows were going to do the job. I had no idea of how many times he had been shot, I just knew that every arrow had been used multiple times and all of my dogs were in extreme danger of getting hurt or killed. They were doing everything anyone could have expected from them and the only way I could see to stop this was to use my gun. I knew that both of these guys were expert and even professional level bow hunters, and if Jim could kill this bear with an arrow he would definitely get a high score in the Pope and Young record book. But all of his arrows were damaged and now he was completely out. I had a great deal at stake here and the last thing I wanted to see was more injuries or even lose one or more of these dogs to this bear, so I told Jim that I needed to shoot it. Just as I was saying this, George rushed over with one more arrow that he found laying on the ground and handed it to Jim. "Try this one again." It looked good enough to try, and I told Jim that this was it, the last one. If it didn't do the trick, I was going to shoot it. So here we go again, with dogs all over him and the bear still charging and running every one of them down, Jim ran right up to within arms length of it and with a quick draw and release, that was it! This last arrow went right up to the feathers and within less than a minute, it was over.

I was impressed with both of these guys for the courage they displayed that day, courage that not many would have shown under similar conditions. Jim was an excellent shot, almost lightning fast to reload and release again and never hit a dog or missed the bear. He stayed right up close to it and shot into the tight spaces between every dog, as the whole pile of them, was moving in every direction. Spot was the only one with injuries bad enough to need stitches, and he got about sixty of them that day. It turned out that the Broadhead's Jim was using on his arrows were all experimental, and had never been tested before. But all and all, it worked out just fine and after skinning out the bear we headed to Redding. Both of the bears Jim and George took in those five days were big enough to be entered in the Pope and Young record book and because of all the excitement, Jim ended up writing his own story about the hunt which was published in the June of 1971 issue of Bow & Arrow Magazine.

Myself with Spot

You can easily see part of the injury to Spot's back leg.

Close calls like this can easily turn into life or death injuries, and Spot had his share of cuts, bruises, and even broken bones. But then when you have a dog that is always baying a bear nose to nose, things like this should be expected. That was the way Spot did it, and thanks to him having a good support team along with him, he didn't get killed doing this; he came close, but never killed. Once a bear runs a dog down and gets on top of it, it will be lucky to get out from under it alive, much less, without any injuries.

I took Spot to the same hospital that most of the hound hunters in that area used, and after the vet put Spot on the table, he kind of stepped back, looking at him, and asked me, "Don't I know this dog?" He knew him all right, and it wasn't the first time he had ever used a needle and thread on him. The doctor was a pretty neat guy, really liked hounds, and he said that it seemed like most good bear dogs would usually need a stich or two from time to time. He was right, they sure do. Unfortunately, some of these hard hitting bear dogs get hurt so bad that they will need more than just stitches.

Things were beginning to look up for me and I was ready for it, especially with all the changes coming about in California. Since I had added bear hunts to my portfolio I was actually making a little money. So much so, that I was able to purchase a three-acre parcel of land in Glennville where I first built a barn, had an outstanding horse and my great group of dogs. My success rate was just a little below a hundred percent for everything I hunted. I still lived in the old house where I had kept the lions behind the garage, but with the changing of the lion's from predator to game animal, I couldn't do that anymore, which was fine, because I actually preferred the new law.

I was still able to guide and hunt lions in California with some success, though I was finding myself spending more and more time in Utah and Nevada for that. By this time, there had been several featured articles written about my hunts in well-known magazines, and this was helping to bring in more customers. The one Jim Dougherty wrote was the second one about my bear hunting in Northern California and I was pleased with it. The first article featured a successful bear hunt in Trinity County with Jim Bridges and Mel White, in 1968. Mel was the associate editor at Western Outdoors Magazine, with the story title, "Dog Creek Bear Race," This came out in the November 1969 issue. I started getting many more requests from bow hunters who wanted to hunt with me, and I enjoyed taking them; all bow hunters I had met so far were very good sports and in pretty good physical condition, both of which were very important when it came to following the hounds.

Hall of Fame Archery Hunter, Jim Dougherty, with George Wright and the Pope and Young record book bear that Jim killed on this hunt. At the time this bear placed in the top 5 of California killed bears. This turned out to be a very exciting hunt with two outstanding, professional archery hunters

Chapter 14

FROM DEVIL'S KITCHEN TO BULL RUN

1972 AND 1973 WERE EXCEPTIONAL YEARS FOR MY BEAR HUNTS, AND ONE OF THE THINGS THAT I REALLY LIKED ABOUT THIS PART OF THE SOUTHERN SIERRAS WAS THAT DURING THE SPRING AND SUMMER MONTHS, BOBCAT HUNTING WAS EXCEPTIONALLY GOOD HERE. To me, this was one of the best ways to train young dogs and it also kept all of my dogs in the best of shape while the bear seasons were closed. Usually, I would return from Nevada lion hunts by late April or early May when the grass had turned green, the trailing conditions were at their best, and there were plenty of bobcats to run.

It was mid-May and I was hunting in the Alder Creek, in the Greenhorn Mountains when my dogs started trailing something that had passed through the Alder Creek campground. The scent wasn't very fresh and looked like it had not been there for several hours. The dogs were moving toward the western side of Red Mountain, which was to our south. There were no roads in this area, so the only way to follow them was on foot. I couldn't find any tracks from the animals they were trailing, but I was sure that it wasn't a bobcat. They had cold-trailed it for over one mile when they jumped it and didn't go much further before I could hear them baying it.

When I caught up, they were at the head of a canyon called Bear Creek and it definitely wasn't a bobcat. Of all things, they had a bear bayed up, and it didn't look like the old guy was going to make it easy on them. They had him surrounded as he was standing in a large pool of water about thirty feet in diameter and three feet deep. The only time he came out of the water was when he tried to catch a dog. He would run out after one of them while the others would put him back into what was now becoming a mud hole. At the same time, they knew better than to go in after him while he was standing almost shoulder deep. I could see that he was somewhat different than most bears by the way he would single out one dog at a time and then lunge at it. This made it difficult for me to put a stop to things and get out of there without anyone getting hurt, including myself. Plus, I had no gun with me, or anything else to protect myself in the event he came after me. All I could do was catch one dog at a time, and only then when they got close to me. This bear was larger than most, and his entire body was black, except for a white patch on his chest shaped like the letter H, and he wasn't afraid of dogs. So I started gathering each dog, one at a time, while keeping my distance from the bear. As soon as I had all of them on a leash, I left him in the mud hole and headed for my truck.

There were a few other hound hunters that hunted in this same area and over the next few months I was hearing stories about this old bear. He was starting to get a reputation as an extremely mean bear. There were several hound hunters who tried catching him only to find that instead of running from the dogs he would try to catch their dogs. I heard stories about him running an entire pack of dogs back to the guys' truck and even put their owner into the cab of his truck.

The next time that I saw him was on a hot summer morning in the month of August. I was exercising my dogs on the Sandy Creek Fire Road, and it was about ten in the morning, and the temperatures climbing fast. It looked like it was going to be a scorcher by the end of the day, and I was simply letting my dogs run ahead of me while I followed in my truck. I was hoping to have them go for about four or five miles and then load them up and head back home. I thought that since it was late morning, they wouldn't be able to smell anything that had crossed the road during the night, so this was intended to be an exercise outing only.

We had only gone about a mile when all of a sudden, they all picked up the scent of something and bailed off the west side of the road and headed down hill. I immediately started looking around, trying to see if I could find any tracks in the road but the dirt was so hard I could barley see tire tracks much less an animals track. There was no way I could see anything by looking at where the dogs had gone down, then on the opposite side of the road I found where a bear had come from above, crossed the road and continued down hill. At first it didn't look like it was all that fresh of a track, but what little I could see, it looked to be a pretty good size bear. When the dogs first left the road it didn't sound like they were going to have much luck catching up with it, but then all of a sudden one of the dogs started to baying, and it sounded like it was looking right at it. That only lasted for about thirty seconds when all hell broke loose. There was no doubt about it, they caught up with this bear and within only a few minutes the fighting went to baying. It was easy to tell that they caught up with a tough one and it wasn't going to let them take ahold of him and with the hot conditions, they probably weren't going to be able to put enough pressure on to make it climb a tree. By now I was starting to regret having let the dogs out here, but it was too late now. It was already a pretty hot day and only going to get hotter, and by the way this was going I could see this ending up without a bear up a tree, and dogs scattered all over those mountains.

They had been after him for only thirty minutes or so when he made a turn and started walking straight up towards the road and right where I was standing. He was in heavy oak brush when I first saw him, and then when he got about a hundred feet away I recognized him. Here he is, that white letter H stood out like a bright and shinning light. I stepped back out of the way in hopes that he wouldn't see me, and if he continued going this direction, I could catch my dogs as they came into the road. It worked, then as soon as he stepped into the road, he saw me and for the first time since the dogs got after him, he broke into a run and like a flash he was up the hill on the other side of the road and he was gone. As fast as I could go, I grabbed Flipper, then Curley and with the help of a friend we caught the other dogs, and loaded them back into my truck, and the race was over. This was my second time seeing this guy and to be perfectly honest, with what I had seen of him before and with the reputation he had earned in the past couple of months I didn't care if I ever saw him again. Most of the time, it seemed like bears of this type would usually move on when harassed enough by hounds, and find another place to live. But not this bear, he was different. We would be meeting again and when we do, it will not end so quickly.

The summer months here were hot and dry, which was normal for that part of the country, and during the dryer years the acorn crop could be scarce in some places. When that happened, I would have to look harder for areas where there were plenty of acorns, and in one of these isolated areas, I could usually find at least one bear feeding, and sometimes there would be several bears hanging out close by. I usually looked for tracks that had crossed the logging roads first, and if there wasn't anything there, I looked for canyons that had plenty of the oak trees in them in hopes that they were dropping acorns.

By the time the season opened, I would usually know where to get started, and this season I had so many hunters scheduled, I felt I could use a little help during the first two weeks of the season, which started on October fourteenth. So I contacted my friend Louis Strawn, who had been hunting with me off and on for about six years. He had some pretty good bear dogs, plus we saw eye to eye on just about everything, which made for a good working relationship. We both had CB radios in our trucks, which helped us stay in contact with each other as we hunted in separate locations at the same time. I started in Wagy Flats as soon as the season opened and Louis would hunt in the Pine Flat and California Hot Springs area. We would meet at my house in Glennville, each one taking a hunter, and headed out from there each morning. Over the years I had scouted out the Wagy Flat area and it never seemed to be very good for bears, but this year was different—they were everywhere. As soon as the season opened I took about five bears from the Wagy Flat area in about as many days of hunting, and then I decided to give it a rest and return to hunt in the mountains just above Glennville. Louis had a business in the valley where he road sided alfalfa hay, and could only hunt for a couple of days on this trip. He was able to catch a bear for one of my clients in the Hot Springs area and then he had to go back to work again. He left me with his dog Hammer this time, which I would always welcome his help.

I had a couple of bow hunter's scheduled for my next hunt, and right off we got after a bear that treed pretty fast. We started it just a little north of Greenhorn Summit and close to the Black Mountain and the Black Sambo Mine turnoff. From there, the dogs trailed it west towards Sunday Peak, where they jumped it and then dropped down into the upper portion of Cedar Creek, where they treed it in the creek bottom, only about half a mile above the Cedar Creek Campground. This made things really easy; since there was still somewhat of a trail left there that lead straight up the canyon bottom to the old Owl Mine site.

As soon as we got to the Cedar Creek campground we unloaded everything that we needed and headed up the canyon bottom to where the dogs had the bear up a tree. These were some well-seasoned bow hunters and I had no doubts that this would go well; but just to be safe, I still carried my rifle with me. I also knew that all of these bow hunters wanted to get everything that they killed into the Pope and Young record book but to do this, the animal had to be killed by only an arrow.

Where this bear was in the tree should have been an easy shot, however instead of hitting it in the rib area, his arrow hit the bear in the shoulder area. Hitting it there might have caused it to eventually die over time, but this was not what any of us wanted or expected. Then, just as he started to take another shot in hopes of hitting it in the ribcage area, the bear started coming down the tree as fast as it could go, and when it was about fifteen feet from the ground it jumped out on the uphill side and landed right into the middle of the dogs. From there, the bear continued to run up the hillside to the east, with the dogs all over it. After going about two hundred feet, it turned and started back down towards the creek bottom below us. Now only about seventy-five feet away, it made a quick right-hand turn and headed straight at us. This all took less than fifteen seconds and then here it came. With its head stuck out as far as it could stretch its neck, and running as fast as it could, it was coming straight at us. Then, as fast as I could point and shoot, I shot it in the head and that was it. This happened so fast that I actually fired my rifle using only one hand and it was so close to the end of my rifle barrel when I pulled the trigger that the bear actually had powder burns on its hair. Shooting this bear was something that I didn't want to do, but there was no question in anyone's mind that if I hadn't done it, someone was going to get hurt; And it looked like that person was going to be me.

Needless to say, both of these bow hunters were shocked, and their eyes were as big as they could get. At that moment they didn't care about Pope and Young records anymore, they were just happy that it didn't get ahold of anyone. I told the guy who first shot it with the arrow that I knew it would no longer qualify for the Pope and Young records since it had also been shot with a gun, so I said that if he would like, I would tag this one for myself and catch him another one. But his answer was, "No Way." He wanted this one. He didn't care about size or records. This had been too exciting to let it go anywhere except home with him.

The next day we headed out to hunt around the Sandy Creek Fire Road. We were now having windy conditions and it didn't look like the trailing conditions would be very good, but we were going to give it a try anyway. This was close to where I last had seen the mean old guy with the white letter H on his chest. It had been about two months since I last saw him and I had figured he had moved on and had forgotten all about him.

The ground was too hard to see any tracks unless they were going up a steep bank, so I turned Flipper loose to hunt the road ahead as we slowly followed him in the truck. We started at Sandy Creek, then after crossing Telephone Ridge we went down to Peel Mill Creek and came up with nothing. This didn't surprise me at all, because the Santa Ana winds had come in and were blowing hot and dry air throughout the area making it very difficult for dogs to smell anything well enough to trail. It was daybreak by the time we stopped at the Peel Mill Creek crossing, then I told my hunters to stay put at the truck while I took the dogs up the creek. If I got anything going, I would call them on the radio, otherwise just stay put. They were game, so off I went.

I had only let Flipper loose to start, and we had gone only about a hundred and fifty yards when he struck a track and started going straight up the creek bottom. The wind was still blowing so hard that I knew it had to be fresh, so I turned all the other dogs loose with him and up and out of hearing they went. I called these guys on the radio to see if they had heard the dogs, but they hadn't. So I asked them to move my truck down the road about a mile and a half to where the road went around to the other side of the ridge, and listen from there while I climbed the hillside to the north and onto Peel Ridge, where I thought I might be able to hear them.

It took me about twenty minutes to make the climb and as soon as I got there, I could barely hear the dogs. They sounded like they were heading northeast towards Marshall Meadow and Peel Peak, about an air mile away, and across one deep canyon. At the time, there were no roads to Marshall Meadows, so there was only one way to get there, and that was to walk. I felt that if I went back to the truck I might not be able to locate them again because of the lack of roads in the area where they were headed, so I headed on up the trail, hoping to find them somewhere around Marshall Meadows.

The trail was steep but easy to follow, and it was easy to tell by the constant roar coming from the dogs they were after a bear, and one that would rather fight than climb a tree. I kept going as fast as I could and after a 1,500 foot climb in elevation from where it all started, I was passing through Marshall Meadow and onto the east side of Peel Peak. I was sure that they had come through here less than an hour ago, but I couldn't hear them anymore and I had no idea of where they had gone. I kept going north, past Peel Peak, heading toward Spear Creek, when all of a sudden I could hear the dogs again. This time they were across several canyons to the north and to the east of where I was. It sounded like they were now about a mile above me, and very close to Portuguese Pass and still baying hard. As I listened I could tell that they were now heading west and into Spear Creek. Then all of a sudden they broke loose, and were coming down Spear Creek so fast that they were in a dead run. And for the first time since this all started, I thought that the bear had probably had enough and after a short run he would look for a tree. But instead, they all faded out of hearing as they went straight down this canyon.

I was in an area that I knew quite well, having treed lions, bears, and bobcats from one end to the other. Where they were now, the canyon walls were almost straight up and down, full of brush, rocks, and just about everything that helped a bear to fight off the dogs. But the farther down it went, the more it opened up, it actually became easier for the dogs to put on the pressure. If he would only head into that area, I figured they would tree him. I was lucky to have heard them when I did because it was only for a few seconds and then they were gone again. I could tell they were heading down Spear Creek, so I followed. The next time I heard them was about an hour later when they had crossed the Bull Run Trail and went around the north side of Sugarloaf Peak. By then it was close to 1:00 PM, which put the dogs at chasing after the bear for around seven hours. Seven hours: that's too long to expect that they would tree him. I had seen bears go up a tree after a few hours of hard running, but that's not what was going on here.

After this many hours, I was surprised and impressed that they were all still together and baying him like they really mean it, especially with Curley and Mindy being only two years old. From there I kept heading cross-country and downhill, all the way to the Sugarloaf Road. Once I got there I was back to having no idea of their whereabouts; I only knew they had been going in that direction when I last heard them. I was about halfway between Sugarloaf Village and Sugarloaf Lodge, and I was standing in the road when I got a call on the CB radio from Louis, who was trying to find me back on Sandy Creek Fire Road. I was surprised to hear from him since I knew he had to work that day. He told me that as soon as he finished his work he returned to the mountains to see what I was doing. No one had heard from me since 6 AM and it was now almost 3 PM. Louis told me that he was able to talk with my hunters who still had my truck and were now at Panorama Heights Lodge. He continued telling me that he had heard my dogs about an hour earlier and they were down in the bottom of White River, somewhere between Observation Point and the White River Campground. He then went on to tell me that it sounded like all five dogs were still together. He stayed put, listening to them until they faded out of hearing as they went down and into the White River Canyon Gorge. After hearing that, I felt this had now gone from bad to the worst place for these dogs to be running a bear, and the chances of them ever treeing or stopping it was not very good. Louis asked me to wait right where I was and he would come get me, A.S.A.P.

I knew it would take a while for him to find me and then get down to the lower road where he had last heard them. This would take too long, and I wasn't going to just wait around, so I decided to keep moving. I told Louis where I was going and maybe he could find me later. I left there as fast as I could go, and headed down the road to Sugarloaf Village, got onto Bear Trap Ridge, followed it downhill for about three miles to the White River road, and as soon as I got there I could finally hear the dogs again. I could hardly believe what I was hearing. At that point it had been more than ten hours and all five dogs were still together. They had chased that bear over fifteen air miles through some very rough, straight up and down terrain. They had started at an elevation of about 5,000 feet, crossed over a bunch of deep canyons, climbed to as high as 7,000 feet at Portuguese

Pass, then dropped back down below White River Campground, which was at an elevation of about 4000 feet. From there I located them as they were coming out of White River Canyon and heading south on the west side of Lone Pine Creek. They had apparently run him all the way through the gorge, before getting where they are now. They were showing no signs of giving up, and neither did I. We were a team, and just like I expected them to stay after everything they got after, I knew that they expected that somewhere along the way I would show up. Needless to say, I was beyond tired but, this is the closest that I have been to them since they pulled out of Peel Mill Creek and I couldn't give up.

They were still in the White River Canyon drainage and a little over three air miles west of the campground where Louis had heard them and less than a mile below where I was now at. From there I went about half a mile to the south on the White River Road and headed west on a ridge that separates the river from the Jack Ranch area. On the northern slope of this ridge, where I could hear the hounds, was very a steep canyon covered with thick brush and rocks. This made it a perfect place for a bear to fight off or even run down and catch the best of dogs. From the highest points to the Canyon bottom is a drop of about 2,500 feet, and they were about halfway from the top and still heading southwest. They were still baying hard, and knowing those dogs, I was sure that when they were given the opportunity, some of them would try to get a mouthful, which would usually put any normal bear on the run or up a tree. But this bear was anything but normal, and it was obvious that there was no way he was climbing any tree. I was sure that thought never crossed his mind. He would much rather fight.

Before leaving the road, I paused only a moment to pinpoint their exact location and once I had that, I took off after them and traveled along the top of the same ridge that they were coming up to. I continued to stay above them as best I could, while they were still in the brush and rocks below and going over one hogback after another. This ridge I was on had very little brush on it and was mainly covered with oak and pine trees, which helped me to cover ground much faster than I could if I had been at the same elevation as the dogs and bear. After moving as fast as I could go for about thirty minutes, I was only one small hogback ridge behind and within three hundred feet above them. It was hard for me to believe what I was actually witnessing here; they were hammering him with one attack after another and baying so hard that it sounded like they were about to rattle the acorns right out of the trees.

As I got closer, I could tell they were coming up a draw just next to the one where I was, so I moved over to that one, and waited to see where they would go next. I could tell that this bear was just walking and neither it nor the dogs knew I was there, and they were heading straight up the same draw that I was in! And suddenly, there he was, black as coal and less than fifty feet below, he was heading straight towards me. The brush was so thick that the dogs had to be within five-feet of it to even be able to see him. As they came up the hill, Flipper was on his left and Hammer was on the right, with the other three dogs right behind him. Every one of them was baying as hard as they could. Then he saw me standing right in his path my rifle raised shoulder high and ready to shoot. After seeing me, and within a split second, he raised his head up and whirled around on just his back feet. As fast as he could turn to his left and knocking Flipper down and under him, then he lunged straight through the dogs that were directly behind him. At the same time, and just as he was completing his one hundred and eighty degree turn, Hammer grabbed him by his left shoulder and was now hanging on to him as he was heading back down the hill. At this same time Flipper came rolling out from under him and grabbed him by his right back leg. The other three dogs got out of his way as fast as they could, which gave him all the room he needed to run straight through them and back down the hill, only this time he had two dogs hanging onto him. This all happened in the time it takes to blink an eye, but before he completed his turn, I was able to recognize who he was by the white letter "H" between his front legs. I wasn't surprised, not one bit. It was him, the badass from Alder Creek.

I knew him all right, and so did every other hound hunter in the Alder Creek area. This was the guy that once chased a hunter back into the cab of his truck while his dogs hid underneath. I was surprised that I hadn't yet lost one of my own dogs to him. There was only one-way to stop this never-ending hunt: I had to drop him right then or there. There was no way of knowing where he would run off to. I was left with a difficult decision, and absolutely no time to think it over. I had to take a wild and very risky chance at shooting him without hitting any of my dogs. As mentioned before, Flipper had him by his right back leg and right next to his tail, Hammer had a mouth full of bear hide on his left side, while the others gave him room to run. When it came to taking a shot at him, this was a little more than just shooting at a moving target. He was running wide open down hill, with two of my dogs hanging onto him, and I can't hit any of these dogs. So, I aimed my rifle less than a foot above Flipper's head and pulled the trigger. The bear took a hit just to the side of his backbone, and the fight was on again. Down they went as fast as ever, with the hounds all over him in a wide open race and heading for the bottom of the canyon. If it wasn't for him carrying a .35 caliber slug somewhere in his back, I don't think I would have had a chance at another shot.

This bear was already mean, and now I had a mean bear that was wounded. These dogs didn't seem to care how mean he was or how thick the brush was; they were going crazy and were all over him as he ran down the mountainside. They only went about five hundred feet before he stopped to fight. I took out after them, and I kept my distance at the same time as I ran past them and got in front of their path. After about a three minute standoff, they all started running down hill again. It looked like they were going to catch up with me, so I found a clearing about a hundred feet long and fifty feet wide, it was right in the bottom of this draw that he was in. It was a perfect spot to ambush the bear if it would only keep coming. I waited and within about thirty seconds, there they were.

It was my last chance. He was less than a hundred feet away, running as fast as he could go with the dogs at his heels. It had to be quick. There was no time to do anything except aim and shoot. I raised my rifle, aimed just a little in front of his right shoulder and dead center with his body as he was running by me, and fired one shot. I knew that I had hit him again, and this time he didn't go far, maybe another fifty feet. He stopped, rocked back and forth on his feet for a few moments then, he fell over onto his side. He was finally dead.

As I walked over, the dogs started to maul him, but as soon as they would grab ahold of him, they would let go. They knew he was bad and they weren't yet sure if he was really dead. This only lasted for a few seconds, and then when they knew he was dead, they had their way with him. I knew it was getting late in the day, and when I checked my watch I could see that the sun would be gone in about twenty minutes. That gave me only a few minutes to peel this hide off of him. At the time, I could usually get the hide off of a bear within twenty minutes, not counting the skinning of the head, feet, and toes, and that's just what I had left to do it. I got the hide off of him just as it went dark, and then I threw it over an Oak limb so it could air out, and cool off during the night. I took a good look around before leaving so I could remember where I left it, and then I would return in the morning to pack it out.

I knew I had a long way to go to get back, and the only light that I had to help me find my way would be coming from the stars and moon above. I was fortunate that the skies were clear and everything was shining as bright as ever. I knew the area well, so I snapped the dogs up and started climbing straight up. It was going to take a while to get back on the main ridge again and that would give me some time alone to think about my two bow hunters, and of course, the day's events.

Here I had two nice guys who came to me in hopes of killing a bear with their bows and arrows. Helping them do this was my priority, and so far it hadn't worked out so well. I knew that I needed to give the dogs at least a day's rest before hunting them again, and I also had to go back for the hide the next morning, so that ruled out the next day. I also knew that it wasn't my fault that these last two bears were the way they were, but I still had an obligation to send my hunters home with two bear hides. I couldn't help thinking about the bear I had just killed. It would have been a special trophy to anyone. That old guy was rough and tough that's for sure. He would have easily pressed the scales at about 325 to 350 pounds, field dressed, he had great color, and a reputation as the meanest bear on the mountain. I knew he was all of that, but in my eyes, there was more to him than that. He was special and I respected and even admired him. I felt the same way about the dogs walking alongside me; it would be hard for me to put my feelings about them into words.

I kept pushing forward, and it was 10 PM when we reached the ridge. As soon as I turned on my CB radio, I heard Louis trying to find me. I told him where I was at, and within minutes I was loading my dogs into his truck and we were exchanging stories. It had been sixteen hours since I turned the dogs loose and I needed to get home. The bow hunters were at my house when I got there, Louis dropped me off and headed for his place in the Valley, and I fed my dogs and myself, and then crashed hard, I was *beat*.

Louis came back the next morning and picked us up at eight. Then we all went back to find the oak tree where I had hung the hide. Louis knew someone who owned a ranch not far from where I had killed the bear and they said it would be okay with them for us to come out to their place instead of packing it back up to the ridge. At the time, I had no idea of just how far down into the canyon I was when the hunt had ended, but I was a lot closer to the bottom than I realized. I had killed it close to a place called Devil's Kitchen, of all things, and when we walked out to the ranch house on White River we met some cowboys who said that they heard the dogs and the final shot from their corrals.

I felt bad about killing both bears while these two were hunting with me, so I offered to give this hide to the other bow hunter if he wanted it. But he declined and said that if anyone deserved this one it was me. I was very glad to hear this, since deep down I felt the same way. It had been one of the longest bear races I had ever experienced, and I was sure that if I could flatten out all of the mountains, ridges, and canyons that we had covered, it would probably have added up to around twenty- five miles of actual travel.

These two guys had only been scheduled to hunt with me for three days and their time had run out by the time we went to retrieve the bear hide. But then the hunter who I had scheduled for the next two days called and cancelled. I asked them to stay at least one more day so I could catch them another bear, and they gladly accepted the offer. Louis couldn't come, so the three of us headed out the following morning to hunt in the southern end of the Sandy Creek Fire Road. By the time we reached McFarland Creek the dogs were already after a medium-sized bear. It was heading up into the Bohna Peak area when the dogs jumped it just a below this huge outcropping of rocks. From there they ran it into Cedar Creek and treed it. Of all things, this bear ran up a tree in almost the same place where I shot the one just three days earlier. These guys were really pumped, and fortunately the kill was quick and clean—one arrow and that was it.

My next hunter came in only two days after they had left. He was yet another bow hunter. Leo Farley was well known among a particular group of Southern California hunters with whom he had accomplished a lot, and I was looking forward to hunting with him. I had taken his dad, Red Farley, on a hunt in Nevada earlier that year. Old Red was quite the character, always telling tales about something. And little did I know, he was a first-class horse trader, to say the least. He stayed with me for about five days, but the hunting conditions were not working in our favor at all, and I couldn't find a lion for him. But Old Red was not about to go home empty-handed. Before I knew it, Red had traded me out of my sawed-off .30-.30 Winchester rifle, one that I owned before I was old enough to shoot it. When I had started hunting with the hounds, I took it to a gunsmith and had them cut the barrel down so it would be easier to carry through the thick brush of the California coast. What I got in exchange was a brand new Marlin lever-action .35 caliber rifle that shot about six inches too high at close range. Believe me, I was regretting the trade from the moment we exchanged rifles, but a deal was a deal. There is more to that story, but I turned my attention to Red's son Leo and our search for a trophy-sized bear.

I had recently seen some big tracks in the higher elevations above Glennville, so I thought that was where we should start. It wasn't always the easiest place to tree a bear because there were some pretty steep and deep canyons, and once you left the top there weren't many roads to help with following the dogs. It could be a real problem if a bear decided to dive off into one of those places. I was comfortable with going there after meeting Leo, and he looked to be in pretty good shape, so the next morning we were heading to the Greenhorn Summit, then turned north and hunted from there looking for bear signs all the way to the northern end of Tyler Meadow but, so far there was no sign of anything.

Then we turned onto the road that goes to Baker Point, and as we were crossing over Tobias Creek we could see where a very large bear had walked onto the road from below, out of the creek. It had then gone up the road the same direction we were headed, toward Baker Point. The tracks were much larger than average and all we could hope for was it wouldn't double back into the difficult terrain from where it had come. It was almost impossible to follow dogs in that area, and I couldn't chance losing them after all they had been through in the past week. If the bear did that, then I'd have to pass and let it keep on going.

Then, we started following him and after going only a short distance he turned to the south, and left the road heading towards Bull Run Basin. So far it looked good, so I first tried Flipper just to see how fresh the track was and when he went out running at full speed, I immediately started turning all the dogs loose and in no time they were all out and heading straight down into the basin. The next time we heard them, they were heading to the east side of the basin and climbing up Baker Ridge, and then they crossed right over Baker Ridge and disappeared as they went into Stormy Canyon. This whole thing took less than thirty minutes and they were gone. This was the last thing that I wanted to see happen, and now all we could do is hold tight and wait to see what might happen. I started to explain to Leo that where the dogs are now, in a canyon that is appropriately named Stormy Canyon with no roads, no trails, full of thick brush, and almost straight down for about one mile in elevation, where it bottoms out at the Kern River, I was concerned. At certain times of the year this area was almost always good to find both bears and lions, but there was always a chance that something like this can happen. We then drove up the road towards Baker Point and listened there for a few minutes, but nothing. From there we drove back to where we turned them out, and then, all of a sudden, there they were. They were coming back across Baker Ridge about a mile further south of where they crossed the first time and running as hard as they could. They crossed back over Baker Ridge and went straight into the bottom of Bull Run again. From there they headed west for about three miles and ran at full speed across the basin, then faded out of hearing as they disappeared up Shultz Creek. This was good; there was a road that went around the upper portion of Shultz. Without wasting any time, we jumped in the truck and in less than fifteen minutes we were there. But no dogs! What happened? It didn't make any sense. The way they had been running I expected to find them treed here. Instead, there was only dead silence. It was like they had totally vanished.

First thing we thought was that while we were driving over there they must have kept going up Shultz Creek and crossed over the main backbone of the Greenhorn Ridge and then down the other side toward Spear Creek. That was only about two miles beyond where they had been, so we headed out to see if we could find them on the other side. The drive took about an hour, round trip, but we had no choice, and when we arrived, they weren't there, either. Surely they hadn't quit, and just let the bear go. No way, those dogs didn't do that. So, where were they? They were out there all right and they were most likely looking right at a big old bear that was either treed or still running from them. The only logical answer was that we'd been looking in the wrong places. So we needed to start looking elsewhere, and fast.

They couldn't have gone back across the basin and over Baker Ridge or we would have heard them from where we were. The only thing left was for them to have gone down Bull Run Creek; it was the only thing that made any sense. But if they did, it would be almost impossible to find them, especially if they had gone very far down the canyon.

It was getting close to noon and we needed to get a move on if that's where they were. We needed to find someplace where we could listen off into Bull Run Creek where it turns to the east and heads towards Kernville. So we drove out on the road between Shultz Creek and Deep Creek. After walking the road for a while and listening very carefully, we found only one spot where we could barely hear them, less than fifty feet in either direction. We were lucky; they were several miles away, but we could hear them, and it sounded like they were treed and thankfully only about half a mile down from where the mouth of the canyon begins on its western end. Anything beyond that, and they just would've been gone; that part of Bull Run continues east through a crooked, steep, brush-covered canyon where the walls are extremely steep on each side, with no roads or trails.

But we were in good shape now, and it looks like we found them. Now we just needed to find the best way to get down there. Not far from where we could hear the dogs there was a trail that went down Shultz Creek for about a mile and joins Bull Run Creek. From there, we needed to go another two miles, then we'd have to leave the trail and follow the creek bottom for an additional mile or so, and hopefully the dogs would still be there. I thought it would take us an hour or so to get to where we thought we could hear them. Sure enough, an hour later, we came upon all five hounds barking under a big live oak tree with a huge black bear perched on a branch, and only about twenty feet off the ground.

It looked like it was going to be an easy, clean kill for a bow hunter. We tied the dogs away from the tree so they wouldn't get hurt. Then, Leo lets one go, and hit the bear right in its side where his lungs are located . But the arrow barely pierced its hide; it just stuck there a moment and then fell off. At about the same time the first arrow hit the ground, Leo took another shot only this one went in so deep that only the feathers remained showing. Less than a minute later, the bear dropped from the tree, and was dead before it hit the ground.

I was relieved. When I saw the first arrow hit and fall off, it was a grim reminder of when Jim Dougherty shot an entire quiver of arrows at a bear before one went deep enough to kill it. The big difference was that Jim had been trying out some experimental Broadheads, while Leo was using the old standby, solid metal Broadhead. After this happened, I asked several other bow hunters if they had ever experienced anything like this, their answers were all, no. Leo gave me that arrow, which I still have today, and when most people take a look at it they are surprised at how the rib of the bear had collapsed its point. We skinned him out where he fell and I packed the ninety-plus pound hide back to my truck. At the time, that bear placed fifteenth in the Pope and Young record book and eighth for California.

I want to point out that some of the equipment malfunctions Jim and Leo experienced were no reflection on either of their abilities. They were both excellent marksmen—quick and accurate with their bows, and very knowledgeable hunters. I not only liked them, but also respected them and their abilities. Unfortunately, they have both passed away, but they are not forgotten.

When the 1973 bear season ended, the combined closure of lion hunting and shortening of the bear season put an end to all to my hunting in California. By May of 1974, I would be leaving California and Nevada behind as well and moving to Montana. In the last seven years I had successfully guided hunters in the states of California, Nevada, and Utah, but those states were all putting the squeeze on what I loved to do. If I wanted to continue guiding full time, it was time to go.

When I first started bear hunting, we were allowed to take two bears per hunter per year in certain parts of California. Then in 1969 it was reduced to only one per hunter, a change I actually agreed with. The season started on the second weekend of September and continued until the end of December, which was rarely a productive month, especially the last two weeks. The season was then cut back in 1972 by dropping September altogether so it didn't start until around the third weekend of October. This change removed some of the most productive days of the entire season, and greatly reduced the time I could guide hunters.

Then came the selling of bear gallbladders for use as an aphrodisiac, a popular practice in Asian communities both here and overseas. Along with it came an increase in poaching. These "outlaw hunters" paid no attention to any hunting laws. Some killed as many bears as they could find, whenever and wherever they could find them; allowing a treed animal to go free never entered their mind. And of course, all this began to paint hound hunting in a very unpleasant light, regardless of the hunters who followed all the rules, they were all viewed to be the same. Since we could no longer hunt mountain lions with hound dogs, the animal rights and wildlife protection groups had more ammunition than ever to use against all hunters. Eventually, in 2013 California Governor, Jerry Brown passed a law making it illegal to hunt bears and bobcats with hounds and put the final nail in the hound hunter's coffin, bringing an end to an American tradition in California.

Over the years, I had hunted with people from just about all walks of life: rich and poor, friendly and unfriendly, good and bad, quiet and loud, arrogant and polite, I even had a young boy that almost shot me, you name it, I had them. I took out a lot of bow hunters, but there were many more who used rifles, or handguns. Then there were a few who just wanted to see how it was done with hounds; so once we caught it, we pulled the dogs off and let the animal go free. There were some exceptional hunters in all categories. However, if there was one group that I enjoyed the most it would be the bow hunters—they accepted success and failure better than any. It seemed that they simply loved being out in the woods more than anything else. If they got lucky and scored by taking the animal they were hunting, it was just a bonus thrown on top of all the other satisfaction they received.

Leo Farley
The larger bear on Leo's right is the one Leo killed in Bull Run Creek.
The one on Leo's left is the one that I killed in Devils Kitchen.
Both of these bears are what I would call, pretty good size.

Flipper

He was a mixed breed of Bluetick, and something else, and came out looking like a Bluetick. He was the third dog that Jim Bridges sold to me. Flipper was all bear dog; solid as a rock, and one of the very best bear dogs that I ever hunted with. He ran a track with medium speed, but what he lacked in speed he made up for in endurance. Flipper died at the end of the 1973 bear season from leukemia. His loss was one of the greatest losses of all to me.

Truly a wonderful hunting hound.

Chapter 15

MOUNTAIN LIONS & POLITICIANS

Just as my success as a Hunting Guide was on the rise, so were the changes regarding lion hunting in California. The anti-hunting groups were pushing for laws, any laws that would bring an end to hunting in California, and they started a big push to protect the mountain lion. In many ways, I was in agreement with some of the things that they were trying to accomplish; but not everything. I agreed with having a season with limits, and Game Wardens that spent more time patrolling the mountain areas, and at least try to put a stop to some of these outlaw hunters. Especially those who indiscriminately killed as much of everything that they could. But these groups, like the Sierra Club and Defenders of Wildlife didn't want seasons, they wanted total protection of just about everything. It was easy to see that if they ever got a good foothold, my career as a professional guide in California would be over. There was no doubt in my mind that the lion population in this state was nothing like it had been during the early years of the bounty days, but endangered, no way. Yes, where I had been living and doing most of my lion hunting, their population was way down from when I first started hunting that area. But given a little time, and if there is enough deer to support them, they will be back. Lions like so many other animals drift with the flow of food, and if the deer population starts to over populate, you can count on it, something will move in and thin them out, and in the west, it's usually mountain lions. Anyway, at about the same time that all this got started, in the late 1960's, I am now having to look elsewhere to conduct multiple-successful lion hunts. I'm not trying to say that there were areas in California that hunts like this could not be done, but I didn't have access or knowledge of these places. So, I started making trips to Utah, which was almost always a good bet. In the winter months they were much easier to find because of the snow, and there were also some good sized lions in certain parts of that state. The down side to going there was, it was a long drive just to get there, and I knew that there was poison placed all over this state. So, I only returned there as a last resort.

In an effort to find somewhere else to hunt that is closer to home, I had always heard that there were areas in Nevada that held a fair amount of lions and I wanted to check it out for myself. Jim Bridges told me that he had given it a try, and although he didn't catch anything, he did find some old tracks of a very large lion close to the town of Austin. So we made plans to meet at the north end of the Big Smokey Valley, set up a camp, and started looking. On that trip we only saw a few tracks and they were too old to try and catch. We were both disappointed at first, but then, we only spent about one week looking, and we both felt that we needed to spend more time checking this out. I had contacted the Nevada Game Department and applied for a guide license just in case I wanted to try again and do some hunting there. Nevada had districts set up for guiding and the only one that was available to me was where Jim and I had explored, and I hoped I would have better luck in the future.

My next trip to the area was in winter of 1968-69. I pulled my camp trailer there along with my dogs and horse in the back of my truck, I rolled in and set up camp on the eastern side of the Toiyabe Mountain Range, and at the mouth of Park Canyon. I was to meet a hunter there in about a week and wanted to be ready for him when he arrived. The terrain in the area could go either way, straight up and down or rolling high desert with pinyon pines and juniper. The higher elevations were at times almost impossible to access because of deep, hard, wind-packed snow. Down where I was, there was little or no snow, so it was almost impossible to see any tracks, so it would be up to the dogs to find a lion to trail.

I told the hunter about the conditions being poor and he was a good sport about it. We hunted for over one week, covering three mountain ranges, and never saw any signs of a lion. Simply finding tracks while driving the roads without any snow was out of the question so I started hunting Bo and Saylor loose, by letting them out where they could hunt the road in front of the truck. We were just a little north from the town of Manhattan, and they had gone only about two miles when they found where a bobcat crossed, and after a short race they treed him in a pinyon pine. This cat was exceptionally large and my hunter wanted to take it, but all he had with him was a high-powered rifle that was way too large to be shooting a bobcat. So I loaned him my .22 mag. Pistol, and after one shot we had him. I skinned it out on the spot and we were on our way again. To this very day I believe he was the largest bobcat that I had ever seen, and don't blame this guy for wanting him. That was all that we caught on this trip, so I started jumping between California, Nevada, and Utah in an effort to keep my lion hunting success rate up, and from early September through mid-November, I went to Shasta and Trinity Counties to hunt bear. I stayed in Kern in Tulare counties until late December, when I finished off the California bear season. During the summer months, I continued to scout different areas to learn something of their potential. Since this kept me going all the time, it was almost impossible for me to answer the phone when prospective clients called me for a guided hunt. So I contacted the phone company and asked if they had some sort of answering machine I could rent. The only thing available at the time was a tape recorder about the size of small suitcase where I could leave an outgoing message for the incoming caller and it would take their messages in return. This was better than nothing, but I still had to be there to listen to the messages. If I was hunting from home it was fine, but when I was gone for weeks at a time, I had to ask friends to go to my house to write down all the information, which they'd relay to me when I had a chance to call.

1969 –1970 ended up being a productive season for me. The bear hunts were very productive in both Northern California and as well at home, and I did well in Nevada, Utah, and in California on my lion hunts.

1969 was the first year that the lion was considered a game animal in California. As pointed out before, I liked seeing this, but there was a lot of strong talk about imposing a moratorium, and that I didn't go along with. Most of this was coming from groups that were completely opposed to all types of hunting. Groups such as The Sierra Club and the Defenders of Wildlife spearheaded most of these efforts and I was sure that if they were to get their foot any further in the doorway, then lion hunting in California would be over, and for good.

At that time, they claimed that there were no more than six hundred lions living in the wild throughout the entire state. There's no way that this statement can be accurate, especially coming from those particular groups, As far as I could tell, there had been no attempt to count any live lions. If there was, I sure wanted to know who, how, where, and when this was done. Even if someone were to attempt such a thing, how would they go about doing it? If they thought that by simply driving down some mountain roads and expecting to see the lions or trying to count all the tracks they found in roads or on trails (that is if they even know what a lion track looks like) would be an accurate way of coming up with an accurate number, then they were fools and so was anyone who bought their story. Believe it or not, they were simply throwing out numbers, numbers that no one else could prove to be right or wrong.

Then here came the Fish & Game. They claimed that they did a study that started in June 1971 and went through December 31 of that same year. That's only seven months. Their findings were to include only nine of the fifty-eight counties in California. They claimed that in these nine counties there were 1,224 living lions there. Plus, they claimed that the largest concentration of lions at that time was in the southern part of Tulare and the northern mountains of Kern counties, which was right where I was living and conducting most of my hunting. In this same report, they claimed that in just four of these nine counties (Madera, Fresno, Tulare and Kern) there was a combined estimate of 729 lions living there. They further went on to state that the hunter success for those who were actually involved in catching lions was estimated that for each ten days of hunting, you could expect to catch one lion. Now doing some simple math; that would amount to someone who hunted fulltime at catching an average of thirty-five lions each year. But, according to State records Jay Bruce, who is the State hunter with the most documented kills didn't come close to having an average like that.

Well, here I am. I had been hunting fulltime in this well-known lion territory for quite a while; and when they said this study supposedly took place, I was the only fulltime guide living here, and I specialized in, and made my living hunting for mountain lions. Prior to me moving and hunting here I was preceded by three well known state hunters, and there was approximately ten percent of all bounties paid for lions in the entire State that came out of Kern and Tulare Counties. None of these state hunters ever matched the averages that they say is possible today. I had frequent visits from the Kern County Sheriffs, Tulare County Sheriffs, and U.S. Forest service personnel, and our local California State Game Warden. If any study had taken place, by anyone or group of people to determine a California mountain lion count, then someone would have shown up in my area, and I never saw anyone. The closest that I came to hearing about such an event was one day our local Game Warden stopped by to make sure that I didn't have any live lions caged up in my garage. While he was there I asked what was going on with the lions and he told me that the Fish & Game had just completed a statewide lion count. He didn't know how they did it, just that they had done this. He went on to tell me that this study included this area that I was living in, and now they know just how many lions there are in this State. No, there was no genuine study done in this area. They were both throwing numbers around like throwing darts in total darkness and hoping their side would win. The Fish & Game Department got caught with their pants down and the Protectionists had the politicians in their pocket. Anyone who was paying attention could see that.

But what good would it have done if they did hold meetings about this? Their minds were already made up. Lion hunting in California was all but over. Also, if the State Fish and Game Department even cared, they should have had enough information at their disposal to have countered these groups, or at least put a stop to the moratorium, which went into effect in 1972. Then a permanent ban on sport hunting of lions in California was put up for the residents of California to decide. In 1990 the California State Legislature got what they wanted, lion hunting in California was over.

That's right, instead of the Fish and Game Department, the legislators were now running the show. These lawmakers meet and had private talks with lobbyists who work for the protection groups who don't like people killing anything, and everyone knows how these lobbyists get their way. So, we lost the right to any kind of mountain lion hunting, even catch and release. Now the only way a lion could be killed legally in California is with a State issued Depredation Permit, and one is left to wonder if the protection groups got all they were after. Clearly not. They had wanted *all* the killing put to a stop, yet between 1972 and 2013 there were 6,175 depredation permits issued, keep in mind that for every depredation permit issued, someone's personal property or someone, was threatened or was killed by a mountain lion. During these years there were 2,816 lions killed, giving an average of just over 68 killed per year, leaving almost half of all permits unfulfilled. The big differences between sport killing and depredation killing is that, none of these lions, or *any* part of them, could be legally salvaged for any reason. Once they are killed they are confiscated by the Department of Fish and Game, and disposed of, which according to them, means they were thrown in a ditch and buried.

The Protectionists stopped the hunting of mountain lions for sport in California, but not the killing. They are still trapped, shot on sight, or run down in the old fashioned way with dogs, killed and then thrown away like so much trash. Let's not forget, these animals were themselves born to hunt down and kill, and anyone who owns livestock, pets, and spends time out in the woods can't be expected to just turn the other way when a lion decides to start killing domestic animals, and even people. It's also hard to expect people to sit quietly by and allow such a lion to be relocated in hopes that it won't do the same thing in its new home. The only way to guarantee putting a stop to this is to kill it. But to do so and then just throw it in a hole is a complete waste, and should not be allowed. Yet that's what happens when the wrong people are put in charge.

There were a lot of people who were very disappointed with the California Department of Fish and Game, but at the same time, I wasn't at all surprised. Here was a State governed agency that had paid bounties on more than 12,000 killed lions over the past fifty-five years, one that also employed several full-time hunters for the sole purpose of killing lions. They also had a slew of California state hunting guides, such as myself, to go to for support, as well as a good number of livestock owners who belonged to the Cattlemen's, and Woolgrowers Associations. The State and U.S. Government trappers who lived and worked throughout the State would also have been happy to help them. Instead of seeking our support, they took the protection groups on alone, and ended up losing control of the lion, and the rights to hunt for it, to a bunch of radical city-dwellers and politicians, to a bunch of people who knew very little, or most likely, nothing at all about this animal and its real population.

This all cast a dark cloud over the California Department of Fish and Game. They let us down, and the ones who thought they were saving the lions had no idea of what would actually take place when the animal's population began to increase again.

Rather than give the mountain lion back to the Fish and Game to govern, the state legislators decided it would be best to let the voting residents in California make the decision. The fate of the California mountain lion hunting is going to be put on a State-wide ballot so that people who don't live in lion country, had never seen one in the wild, and have no idea of what goes on out there could make the decision. Common sense had been thrown to the wind and stupidity had taken over.

So now what? Well here comes the best part. California protection groups, wants to conduct some real serious research programs, so they will know everything that there is to know about lions in this State. This means that they can hire educated elites that want to study mountain lions. I guess that taking the word from professional hunters that have spent years finding, tracking, and actually catching wild mountain lions isn't enough. Then in 1990 a state initiative was passed outlawing the hunting of mountain lions in this State. Along with this proposition 117 created the "California Habitat Wildlife Protection Act". This proposition is intended to acquire land that is to be dedicated as habitat for deer, which are not endangered, mountain lions, which in my opinion has never been endangered, and other endangered species, who ever they may be. My question is, why?

California already has hundreds of thousands of beautiful acreage already set aside for these animals; they are called National Parks, and they go by the names of; Sequoia, Kings Canyon, Yosemite, Lassen, Redwoods, etc. only that's not good enough for them. They want sanctuaries set up right in the middle of large human populations, places like the Santa Monica Mountains, which is surrounded by millions of people and five lane highways going each way, that nothing can safely cross without getting killed.

Then, while Alberta, Canada was paying a bounty to kill off their over sized wolves, our Government was relocating these same wolves into parts of Montana and Wyoming. Since that time they have practically decimated the moose and elk populations in many parts of the northwest. Not only are they responsible for this, they are also killing livestock, pets, valuable trail hounds, and other types of hunting dogs, on an ongoing basis, and now these same wolves have migrated into other states, including northern California.

Now we are hearing this same voice wanting to relocate Grizzly Bears into the forest of California. Here's another animal that has no problem killing humans and livestock. And what is there justification for doing all this? Some say, "Well they need a place to live to." Well, they have one, and I'm sure that the ones who have volunteered to hand these predators over to us are glad to see them go.

By the time Proposition 117 will end, it will have cost California taxpayers no less than thirty million dollars each year for each of these thirty years. If this terminates in 2020 as proposed, it will cost the taxpayers in California at least, nine hundred million dollars, and for what. Plus it will be interesting to see an accurate accounting of where all this money has ended up, when it's over.

Question is, who would ever expect to receive an intelligent, or legitimate decision to come from anyone who was given authority over something that they know nothing about? Common sense should tell otherwise, however this is exactly what has happened with the mountain lions in California.

Chapter 16

NEVADA AND UTAH

On one of my earlier trips to Nevada, as I was passing through the southern portion of the Big Smokey Valley, I noticed that there was a place called Carver Station. I had my horse with me and I stopped in to get some information about buying some hay. The gentleman at the bar told me to go up the valley a ways and on the west side of the road I would find a ranch called Young Brothers, and the guys there would take care of me. I mentioned that I lived in Glennville, California, and asked if the name Carver Station, was by chance, associated with any of the Carvers in Glennville, California, and much to my surprise, he said yes, and he was a Carver. He was busy at the time and actually didn't seem interested in talking about anyone in Glennville, so I thanked him for the help and headed north up the valley.

I was planning to stay on the west side of the valley, and set up my camp at the mouth of Ophir Creek, so I went there first, unloaded my horse and set up camp. From there I headed toward the Young Brothers Ranch. They were easy to find, and when I knocked on the door I was met by one of the boys, Darrell, who was about my age. I told him I needed hay for my horse and that I was hunting in the area, and looking for lions. This immediately lit him up. "Lion hunting," he said, "my dad needs to talk to you. Come on in." He rushed me through the living room and into the kitchen where they were all having dinner, introduced me to his father and mother first, and then the rest of his brothers and sisters. They were just sitting down for dinner and offered me to set in with them. I gladly took them up on the offer and they were all much friendlier than the guy I talked with at Carver Station.

Darrell's father, Chester, told me there was a need for a lion hunter in the area. They raised cattle that roamed on the open range and although they weren't having any problems with lions, he thought they might be having an affect on the deer herd, which wasn't what it seemed like it should be. Mr. Young went on to say that it had been several years since he had heard of anyone hunting for them around there, and they would help in any way that they could. Of course they wanted to know where I lived, and what I did there. I told them that I was a fulltime guide looking for another place to do my hunting. To them this sounded like someone that they needed to have around their part of the country, and from my first impressions, this all sounded great to me. We all had a long and pleasant conversation, just before I left, they told me where I should be able to find places known for lion sightings. They had told me that they have a trailer park of sorts nearby, which had electric power, water, and sewage disposal. Mr. Young said that if I was going to hunt for lions in the area he would let me make camp there for free. All he asked for in return was, "Just get rid of as many lions as possible". I didn't know at the time, but eventually, they offered to sell gasoline to me for one cent per gallon over what they were paying for it, which was about one half the price that the local gas stations charged. What a great surprise! All I wanted was some hay for my horse, and he threw that in, too. I said I'd take it, but not just yet. It all sounded too good to be true.

I didn't stay at first because I wasn't sure if that was exactly where I wanted to hunt. I needed to do some exploring and see what the lion population looked like first before I decided to settle in. I had originally come to check out the Toiyabe, Monitor, and Toquima Mountain Ranges, and was going to start out by checking there first. There was a government lion hunter by the name of Wiley Carrol that lived in nearby Ely, Nevada, and I planned to drive over to his place while on this trip. I had never met Wiley before, but we had traded letters back and forth over the past year, and he seemed to be willing enough to offer me advice. During our visit, he told me that the lion population was nothing like it was only a few years earlier, and from what I had already seen I told him that it wasn't what I expected to see. Wiley also told me that Nevada was getting picky about out of state guides. Anyone who wanted to guide there had to apply for a specific area and, believe it or not, there could be a lot of friction coming from some of the locals. He went on to point out that, all the best spots were already taken, so I would probably be stuck with just the leftovers. I mentioned to him that I was staying in the Big Smokey Valley and the Young's Ranch, and it didn't look very promising. He agreed, there were lions there, but nothing like some of the other places. So I chose to spend most of my time hunting in Utah or right back at home in California. It wasn't until 1971 when I finally started to take hunters to Nevada on a regular basis. It still wasn't what I was looking for, but it was better than nothing, and much better than the Greenhorn Mountains.

By then, I had a great bunch of dogs; if they started out after an animal, I could almost always count on them catching it. I no longer had Bo, but Saylor was now my lead dog and he was trained to hunt on bare ground and it didn't matter what he was after, he could and would do it alone, time after time. A bobcat could stay on the ground for only a few minutes after he had jumped it, and that was something that I never saw in any other dog. Lions were as good as caught if there was just enough scent left to trail. He was also an outstanding bear dog. He could strike one from the road while still riding in the back of the truck and track it from there, all the way to be treed.

After expanding my range to Nevada, I then looked into prospects in a few other states, including Idaho. A friend I had hunted with in California had moved to Salmon, Idaho, and he said there was a very good population of both bears and lions around where he lived. The only problem was that Idaho, like some other Rocky Mountain states, didn't seem to want non-resident guides. Like in Nevada, the state was broken up into districts, and only a limited amount of guides were allowed to take hunters into those areas. This was good for game management, especially for anyone who had the license to guide. But without one, prospective guides had to work for the outfitter who had the license, or try to buy them out. All this ruled out Idaho for me. Montana had these same rules, but the biggest problem for me there was that it was illegal to chase bears with dogs, so that state was ruled out as well. I had hunted a little in eastern Washington but wasn't happy with the results, so it too was out. I had no interest in New Mexico or Arizona. Oregon was putting the squeeze on lion hunting, like California, so I scratched it off the list.

I still wasn't convinced that Nevada was all that I had first hoped it was, but if I was to continue hunting lions, it looked like it was my only choice. One thing it had going for it was the places where the lions could be found were much easier to move through than where I was used to hunting. This was mainly due to the type of terrain, and there was usually snow in winter to trail them. On the other hand, summer hunting in Nevada was almost nonexistent to anyone other than the government hunters who were on call to go after lions that killed domestic animals—mostly sheep. They rarely ate anywhere near as much as they killed; they often killed them just because they seemed to enjoy it. Anyway, for the government hunters this worked out good for them.

Willis Butolph once told me that he did almost all of his lion catching during the summer months when he received calls that there was a lion killing sheep somewhere, such as the time he and I went to help Mexican Pete. We didn't catch the lion that time, but usually when he was called out, he would go right to where he could start trailing one, or many times, catch it right at the kill site; this was a totally different type of "hunting." Ordinarily the most time consuming and difficult part of lion hunting is finding a trail fresh enough to catch it. With these government hunts, sometimes known as depredation calls, the hunter wasn't having to find a lion to catch at all; the trail was right in front of the hunter, and if the lion was still close by, or the trail was fresh enough for the dogs to trail, then they were on their way to another catch. It was still lion hunting, but it was almost like taking the hunt out of the hunting, and it could really add up on the kill reports for some of the government hunters. But it's not always as easy as it sounds, as evidenced by the lion that killed Mexican Pete's sheep where as soon as it was done killing a bunch of sheep, it simply disappeared into the hills.

I resolved myself to stay on at the Young Brothers Ranch throughout this next three winter seasons. As I became more familiar with the three mountain ranges where I was permitted to hunt, I started having better success, but it was never as good as I had hoped. All of the lions were actually quite easy to catch once found except for one: a very small female that spent most of her time on the east side of Toiyabe Range in Jett Canyon, where it emptied out down by Carver Station.

I had a man coming in from Alaska to hunt with me. He was a Taxidermist from Fairbanks who also did some guiding. I was to pick him up at the bus station in Tonopah, about a hundred miles south of the ranch. On my way there, I drove into the mouth of Jett Canyon and saw some tracks that looked to be only a few days old, so I planned to go back in the morning to take a look around. When I picked up my hunter, I told him the plan and he was all for it. He was a nice guy with plenty of experience in the woods and I was looking forward to hunting with him. The following morning as we were driving along the bottom of the canyon, we picked up her tracks as she came into the road from the north and headed straight up the canyon bottom. There was a fair amount of snow all around, so trailing was going to be easy. Not only that, the track had not been there the day before, so it looked like it wouldn't take long before we had this one up a tree. The only road in the immediate area was the one we were on, and it stayed in the bottom of the canyon, so if she started out of there it meant we would be going on foot, and these canyon walls were almost straight up and down.

We followed her up the road for a few hundred yards, and when she turned to the south and headed across the creek, I turned all the dogs loose on her trail and off they went. Saylor, Spot, Thunder, and Sue, took off in a dead run. From there they went only about one hundred yards and started heading up the south side of the canyon and stayed about a hundred feet above the canyon floor. They continued that way for about half a mile and then she started climbing towards the top of the ridge. The further she went, the more it looked like she was aiming straight for the top of the highest peak on the ridge above us. By now I had no choice except to keep going after the dogs while my hunter stayed in the road and hollered for me to go on after them and he would try to catch up as best as he could. It wasn't long before I couldn't hear them anymore, didn't know where my hunter was, so I just kept following them in the snow, which was hard crusted and about knee deep. This went on until I got to the top of the ridge, about 1,200 feet up from the bottom.

When I reached the top of the main ridge the wind was blowing so hard that I had to lean into it just to walk, and the blowing snow was starting to cover up their tracks. I couldn't let this happen because this was the only way I could find them, so I had to push myself as hard as I could. I could see that they were now heading west along this ridge, and then it looked like they were going to drop down into Pablo Canyon, to the west. This is not what I wanted at all, and it was easy to see that if that is where the dogs ended up, I would definitely lose my hunter. The daytime temperatures stayed just a little above zero and nighttime temperatures were as cold as twenty below. It was now close to 3 PM, and I had no idea where these dogs were except that they were somewhere ahead of me and there was no doubt in my mind that they weren't going to stop until they caught it. I continued following the dogs' tracks for about a mile along the ridge. Then they started to drop down into Pablo Canyon. I was right behind them, and after about half a mile, they suddenly turned to the north and started climbing back toward the top again. From there, they went up this ridge about a quarter mile and then started heading back down into Jett Canyon, about three miles up from where it had all started.

This side of the canyon was a dangerously steep drop for about five hundred feet and the snow was hard and wind packed, which was like walking on ice. I had to take a different route than the dogs in many places because of these conditions. For the first time in about six hours, as I was dropping back into Jett Canyon, I could finally hear my dogs again. I could tell they had crossed Jett Canyon and treed about a thousand feet up the other side. It was starting to get dark by the time I reached the bottom of the canyon and to my surprise, I ran into my hunter, right where the dogs had crossed the road. He said he had been waiting there for about an hour, and figured it would be the best place for him to find me. "Okay," I said. "Let's get up this mountain as fast as we can because darkness is closing in on us and we have a pretty good climb before we reach the dogs."

He agreed, but he said he wanted to take a look at my face first; because he knew I had been exposed to the extreme cold all day without any protection, I knew that since he was from Alaska, he was probably pretty familiar with frostbite, and he told me he could see early stages of it on my ears and nose. I said I wasn't as worried about that as I was about my feet and my dogs. I had stomped around all day in snow deep enough to get into the top of my boots and my feet were cold to say the least. But I was going to get my dogs as soon as possible no matter what.

The two of us started up the mountainside and within a hundred yards he was falling behind again and by the time I reached the dogs, he had another five hundred feet of climbing to go. I called down to him and asked what was wrong and he said he didn't think he could make it. I told him to sit tight, that I was going to send the lion his way. Then I jumped the lion from the tree, counting on the fact that they usually run downhill after they jump, and it did. But it also ran along the side of the hill and up the canyon and treed again about hundred yards west and a hundred feet above my hunter. I could still call to him and tried to get him to come over where we were, but he yelled back to say he couldn't make it, and asked if I would just let her go so we could get out of there. By then I was ready. It had been dark for about two hours, and I knew that my feet were in trouble. I called to him and told him to get to where my truck was, about two miles down the canyon road, turn on the motor and get some heat going. Then I grabbed up all of my dogs, let the lion go and started down as fast as I could go.

When I got to the truck the heater had not had enough time to get warm, and with the help of my hunter we started getting my boots off. As expected, the water had turned to ice. My hunter took a sleeping bag from behind the seat, wrapped my feet up in it and did the driving. By the time we had hit the main road the heater was pumping out warm air, but when I took the sleeping bag off and tried to expose my feet to the heat, they lit up and burned like the devil. It felt like I just put them into a fire, and I had to keep them away from any type of warm air for about a week. I was about to learn something that my Alaska guide already knew. "Frostbite," he said, "you have a good dose of it." I sure did. I had gotten a minor case of it in California back in 1965, but nothing like this.

In spite of it all, the Alaskan guide was happy. He said that when the lion jumped from the first tree, he was able to see it as it ran across the hills in front of him and that was satisfaction enough for him. There were not many like him, just a good sport all the way around. Together with my hunters, most of them bow hunters, we had taken quite a few lions in the area, with most of them being large males, but just like all the other places I had been hunting in, it was getting harder to find them. Regardless, I couldn't just up and move over into someone else's territory, even if I knew I would find lions there. It's not that I couldn't hunt there on my own, yes, I could do that, I just couldn't guide hunters outside of my area. It was very frustrating that there were other places just on the outside perimeter of my area that had more of everything to hunt for. My friend Wiley Carroll suggested that I take a look at the Ruby Mountains, but there were a few jealous hound hunters that lived in that area so I needed to be careful.

So, one day I decided to go over and hunt on my own in the Ruby Mountains, which were just a little west of Ely, just to see what I could find. Right off on the first day I treed an average-sized male lion. He was an easy catch, so I let the dogs bark at him for about ten minutes, then I turned him loose and went on about my own business. I really liked that area; it was full of deer and much easier terrain than where I had been hunting, but the Game Department told me I couldn't guide hunters there, so I didn't. Then, at the end of the 1972 season I learned from the game warden in Tonopah that the State of Nevada was going to stop all residents from California, specifically, from obtaining guide licenses, starting with the 1972/73 season. Here we go again. Nevada had a reciprocal agreement with other states that would allow them to guide in Nevada for lions in Nevada, but only if the other state would allow Nevada resident to do the same in their state. This ruled me out.

I could still hunt in Utah, but it was a long way to go when the hunts were spaced out weeks apart, so Nevada had become my first choice, and I had learned that it took six months of residency to become eligible to guide there. It seemed easy enough. I was going to be there for more than four months while I hunted for lions, so all I needed was a couple more months and I would qualify. It didn't matter to me if I was a resident in California or in Nevada anyway. So I put in my six months, changed all of my vehicle registrations, driver's license, address, and even registered to vote in Lander County. Once I had established residency, I sent in a renewal application for a Resident Guide License, only this time I requested Region II. I was immediately denied on the grounds that guides could only have one license at a time, and my current license wouldn't expire until June of 1973. Keep in mind, I was sending in my application, dated on their own forms for my new Master Guide License for the following year, only a month before it expired, and this guy in Nevada was telling me that I couldn't have two licenses at the same time. I could smell trouble all over this.

Then as soon as my non-resident license expired, I re-sent in my application for a resident Master Guide License to the Fish and Game

Office in Reno, Nevada. This was in late spring of 1973. By July, I received a letter from their Chief of Law Enforcement, William G. Parsons, who cited commission regulation number fourteen, which stated that since California does not allow a Nevada resident to hunt for lions there, then Nevada cannot issue me a license. I re-sent him proof that I was no longer a California resident and had established residence in Nevada, and pointed out to him that this is my second attempt at obtaining my new 1973-1974 resident Master Guide. I tried calling him on the phone several times, and the results were always, "He's not here." They were obviously messing with me, and it really shouldn't have come as a surprise. Wiley Carroll had warned me that there were resident guides in Region II who wanted to keep all others out, and that even included Wiley, who worked for the government as a federal trapper and lived in Region II. He added that some of them even had political pull, so things could get rough. I didn't care. I needed to get re-licensed, and time was running out.

By September, I was getting ready to start my California bear hunts and I was talking to people who wanted me to take them on lion hunts, but without any place to go, I couldn't book any of them. I continued bugging the people in Reno with phone calls, and all I kept hearing was: "He's not here." Then I finally received a letter from Mr. Parsons, stating the following: "Your application for a Resident Master Guide License has been denied," followed by more quotes from Nevada hunting regulations and section numbers. He went on to cite my "failure to qualify as a resident of Nevada," and added that "an investigation of your qualifications as a resident indicates that you have chosen to become a resident only for the purpose of obtaining privileges not ordinarily extended to non-residences of this state."

I couldn't believe he had actually stated it that way, and he put this in writing. He was right, and I couldn't have said it better myself. I fired a letter right back to let him know that he was exactly right; I had actually become a resident to the State of Nevada for the sole purpose of obtaining privileges not ordinarily extended to non-residents. Then, after a few days, I tried calling him again, and as always, he wasn't there. My next step was to contact the Secretary of the State and Attorney General of Nevada. It was almost December and I should have been booking hunts by now, but I still couldn't do it. Then I receive a letter from Julian C. Smith, Jr., Deputy Attorney General. He was looking into my case and he would call me within a week. When he called, he told me that the Fish and Game headquarters in Reno had issued my license on November 16, 1973, and he wanted to know if I had received it. I said I hadn't yet, but enough time had passed that it should have arrived by then. He told me to call Reno and find out what was going on, and to call him back if they gave me any more trouble.

I called Mr. Parsons yet again, expecting him not to be there, as usual, but I was handed over to the man who actually authorized my license. He said that because of the long delay in issuing my license, the area where I wanted to hunt had been given to someone else and all they could do was give me back the area that I had before. I told him that this was unacceptable and since they were the ones who had delayed this, they needed to issue me the area that I had requested five months earlier. This guy said no! The license had already been filled out and even though it had not been sent, I could take it or leave it. So the Reno office of the Nevada Fish and Game denied me the area that I wanted, which was Region II, said they gave it to someone else and then, they had issued me a license to guide for lions in an area that I had not even applied for. Wiley was right; there *were* politics in lion hunting, I could hardly believe this. Here I was in a state where almost everything seemed to be legal, but Region II was off limits to anyone who wasn't part of the "Good Old Boys Club." I really had no choice except to go back to hunting the same places where I was hunting before, an area that was almost picked clean of lions and looked to be short of deer as well.

As soon as I had finished with the bear hunts in California I was back at the Young's Ranch. Just before I got there, they had a real bad cold spell where the temperatures had dropped to forty below with some very strong winds. This had gone on for more than a week and the Young's were doing what they could to gather up their cattle before the herd froze to death. I tried doing some hunting, but in the beginning it was just too windy and cold to have any luck. They had a hydroelectric plant that they ran on the ranch with their water rights to two creeks that came off the eastern side of the Toiyabe Mountains. The water collected in a dam at the mouth of the canyons, and from there it went underground into an eight inch iron pipe that traveled about one-half mile and dropped about a thousand feet in elevation to their ranch headquarters and generator.

They had never had any problems with the water freezing, since it was always moving to keep up with their electricity and domestic needs, but it had been so cold and for so long that the pipe had frozen almost all the way through. To melt the ice in the pipe, they took a diesel-powered welder and attached the cables to the pipe at about a hundred feet apart, then let the welder run until the iced thawed. They poked a hole in the pipe and let the water drain out to get it flowing again, then welded up the holes, turned on the water, and were back in business.

But before they got this done, they had to pack in water and we had no electricity at all. Fortunately, I didn't have any hunters scheduled, so while I was out looking for lion signs I would also look for any of their cattle that might have gone astray and reported my findings to Mr. Young. Early one morning as I was setting out on my usual rounds, I noticed that the lights were on over at the ranch house, so I went over to see if they needed any help and I was invited in and saw a side of ranching that I never knew about. The entire family was sitting around the kitchen table and they were discussing what each in the family would be doing that day. Mr. Young was the one who was doing all of the talking and everyone was paying attention to him. I was invited to sit in, and as I listened to their conversation, it was easy to see they were worried about this extremely cold weather and their range cows freezing to death. Mr. Young was speaking to his two oldest boys, LeVar, and Darrell. He started off by addressing both of them together by saying that he wanted each of them to take one horse and one dog, he then gave them instructions of the direction that they were to go that day. They would both be riding to the east of the ranch and into the Valley. This could take either one of them onto a ride out about fifteen miles due east and then who knows where. They would ride out together heading due east then LaVar would head north and Darrell would head to the south. Mr. Young told LaVar, that he would drive to a specific location and meet him first around 11:00 a.m. He said he would have a fresh horse for him, make the trade and then head back to the ranch, pick up another horse and do the same thing with Darrell. By now the nighttime temperature had warmed up and was around -15 degrees, or less, and if we were lucky, the daytime temperatures would get as high as 0 degrees. Regardless of the temperatures the wind kept blowing at a pretty good speed, and it was cold.

As soon as Mr. Young was done talking, they got up and started for the door. When they left the ranch they were so wrapped up in heavy clothing and scarfs to protect them from the freezing weather, that there was no way of telling who they were. They both saddled up and off they went. From there we all went off in different directions at the same time, only they were on horses and I was in a heated truck. On that day I hunted in the Toquima Range, which was to the east side of the Valley and besides looking for lion tracks I could also keep an eye out for any cow tracks.

Mr. Young had instructed me to keep an eye out for any cows or cow tracks and he told me that if they were standing with their heads pointing into the wind, they would most likely die. This was something new to me, and something I had never heard of before. Mr. Young went on to explain that when they are facing the hard blowing cold wind, they can get to the point that they can no longer think, especially when the temperatures get as cold as they have been, he said they simply stand there and freeze to death.

As the day was ending and I had not found any signs of missing cows or lions, I returned to the ranch only to find that as I drove up to the end of the main driveway, there were several people gathered together. Mr. Young and LaVar were standing off to the side of the others and it appeared that LaVar was preparing to head out again, only this time with his horse in the back of his truck. As I got out of my truck I was told that Darrell had not returned when expected, and he was now over 2 hours late. This would usually not be of any great concern except it was almost dark, and he had been in the saddle all day, and was now on his second horse, the temperatures were below zero, and the wind was blowing hard. In fact this wind had the snow kicking up with it to where it was so thick that it was almost blinding. Conditions like this can be deadly, especially for someone who could not find any shelter, or has been injured.

The Young's were preparing a search party and they had less than one hour to go before total darkness would set in. LaVar was going to drive to where his dad had last seen Darrell, unload his horse, and start following his tracks on horseback. Mrs. Young had wrapped up some food and drink for LaVar to put in his packsaddle along with a flashlight and extra batteries.

Mr. Young would be driving along any roads that would put him in the areas that Darrell might likely be found in, and I would be doing the same in my truck. Only I would be following the main road and checking to see if he had crossed it. The valley floor to the untrained eye could look like it was flat, but it was anything except that. It was, however, full of gullies, with brush of all types and it could be very hard to locate someone if they were in trouble. Right now, all anyone knew was that it was late in the day, killer cold, and somewhere to the east of the ranch house, there was one lone cowboy, with his horse and dog, but where? He had been in the saddle for about nine hours, and should have been back by now. Then, I will never forget what happened next. LaVar and I were just getting into our trucks and ready to leave, when someone said, "Look!" pointing towards the east I think I might have seen something. "It was almost impossible to see anything because of the blowing snow, but all eyes were trying and hoping for the best. Then about a minute later another one said, "Yeah, what is that?" Next it was just like something taken right out of an old western movie. First there was a cow, it looked like it was heading our way. Then the blowing snow would hide it, but only for a moment or two, and the next time we saw anything, it was a dog following just a little behind it and on it's right side. Then the blinding snow covered them up again. All we could do now was wait, and hope. They were about a half-mile away but they were coming our way, and right behind them was the cowboy we were all so worried about. This relentless wind was coming from the south as he rode towards us, and it was taking the loose end from one of the many scarfs he was wearing and blowing it straight off of his right shoulder to where it was almost level and whipping it like a worn out flag.

When Darrell rode up he was so cold that he could barely move as he slid off his horse, and as he was walking towards the house, all he said is, "I'm almost froze." That's it. No complaints. He was so cold that it was all he could do just to walk, and his face was so cold he could barely move his jaw enough to talk. He just wanted to get warmed up, and he needed to have something warm to eat and drink. As I looked on, I thought to myself, this is a different kind of cowboy, and these are special people.

This winter was devastating to the Young's and by spring they had lost hundreds of mother cows because of the severe conditions, but they were cut from a cloth that not many of us have ever seen. They were first class survivors, knew how to handle tough times, they were also always helpful and kind to me.

Before that winter was over, I would have my own share of problems.

In December 1973, just as I was finishing with the California bear hunting season, my main dog, Flipper, was diagnosed with cancer, and by February I had lost him. This loss to me was another heavy hit. Flipper was a no-nonsense, first-class bear dog that would not give up no matter how tough the bear was, and he would do it all alone. Dogs like him were very hard to find, I knew I was going to miss him for a long time. In the last year-and-a-half, I had lost four of my main dogs, Saylor, Spot, Thunder and now Flipper, plus one other that was a very good dog. They were all in their prime of life, and they all died from assorted medical problems, except for Thunder, who died from injuries inflicted by a bear. Losing any of them was tragic, since each and every one of them were extremely talented hunting dogs, all of which made the losses even greater.

Now, I am back to almost starting over again. My oldest dog was a six year old named Hammer. He actually belonged to my friend Louis Strawn, but because of all my losses, Louis loaned him to me on an almost fulltime basis. All of the others were too young to expect too much from them. Most hunters would have considered this lineup good enough, and I suppose it would have been if I were only interested in hunting for fun. But I was a fulltime hunting guide and they weren't what I considered the best ages to meet my needs. I had no choice except to keep on going with what I had. I thought I would have no problem catching lions with them in Nevada, but it was the mean bears that I was worried about.

As soon as the cold spell came to an end, I was back to hunting again and it wasn't long before I was catching lions.

Then it was my turn to have medical problems. In early February 1974, I was rushed to a hospital in Fallon, Nevada, where I spent two days and two nights so shot up on morphine to the point where I could hardly talk. Then, after the resident doctor realized that the morphine wasn't doing the trick, I was loaded into an ambulance for a seventy mile, forty-five minute ride to the Reno Hospital emergency room. On the way, the paramedic that was at my side was doing his best to keep me from going to sleep, while the driver kept asking him about my condition. All he would say was stable, but I could tell from the tone of his voice that he was conveying to him to keep his foot in it, which he did all the way there. I had no idea how fast we were going, but, with lights flashing and siren screaming, I can still hear the roar of that engine sucking in air all the way. Within thirty minutes after arriving there, I was in surgery. Then two days later I left the hospital without my, almost ruptured appendix.

That ended my season. All the hunters I had scheduled were notified that I was not available for the balance of the year.

Before all this happened, I had been in contact with the Montana Fish and Game and was told that if I could find an area where there were no other outfitters guiding for lions, they could possibly give me a license, but only if I became a state resident. I didn't feel that Nevada was going to give me any of the areas I wanted. I had enough of them, and was tired of fighting for everything I needed. So I studied all of the available areas in Montana, checked out the number of lions harvested each year, and I found that there wasn't anyone doing what I wanted to do in the extreme northwest corner of that state. I sold my house in Glennville, loaded up my stuff in Nevada and headed to Lincoln County, Montana, a place where I had never even been before.

I was leaving behind a lot of memories, most of them good, and I had made many friends all along the way. While I lived and hunted in Nevada and Utah I had learned that not all cowboys, just like hunters, and dogs are the same. I had also learned that there weren't many reasons for me to stay. So it was time for me to say my goodbyes to some of the finest people I had ever known.

1972

Toiyabe Mountains, Nye County, Nevada

From start

This is a typical sight when bare ground trailing lions during the winter, in both California and the southern part of the Toiyabe Mountains of Nevada. Rough, rocky terrain is more the normal than the exception. Thunder is in the lower right corner trying to pick up the scent of this lion while Spot is letting us know that he has found where it was at sometime earlier. We caught this lion, (as seen in the photo below), about one mile from here. Temperatures were well below freezing, with bare ground trailing all the way to the tree. I would say that about a third of all the lions I caught in this part of Nevada, were either started, ended, or both, on bare ground. Nice sized male lion, killed by Bow & Arrow.

The Bowhunter who killed this lion was a boat builder by trade. He said he built them out of concrete, and sold them as fishing boats. A good sportsman, and like most hunters, he was a pleasure to take hunting.

To finish

Myself with Saylor in front and Thunder. It was bare ground trailing all the way and took about one hour for them to catch up to this lion. We never weighed him, but guessed his weight at 145-150 pounds.

1972

Toquima Mountains of Nye County, Nevada

This old boy had to be one of the most beat-up lions that I ever saw. Besides having scars all over his face and body, he was also missing part of his right ear.

We caught him on bare ground as you can see, and he reminded me of the tough old lion that I treed and let go on the Rincon Trail. They were about the same size and carried many similar injuries. We caught him on the western slope of the Toquima Mountains in Central Nevada. He was killed just a little too far from any roads to pack out, so he was never put on a scale. Neither my hunter nor I cared about record book entries so we left the skull right where I skinned it out. Nonetheless, he was big, and I'm sure that it would have easily passed the fifteen inch minimum required for Boone and Crockett.

1972 wasn't the best year for snow in the Toiyabe, and without it, lion catching could be a real challenge. Overall, it wasn't the best place I knew to find and catch bobcats and lions. I found this cat's track one day in just a small patch of snow and wanted to see if we could catch it. As you can see here, we did, and just like everything else for that year: it was bare ground all the way to the tree.

Utah

Nevada

This is typical of the type of trees where I hunted for lions in both Nevada and Utah. I never tried to take any lions alive in Nevada, but I could see that it would be much easier there than it was in most parts of California and Montana, where the lions often got into the taller firs and pines.

Chapter 17

MONTANA

AFTER I LEFT NEVADA IN 1974, MY FIRST STOP WAS THE DEPARTMENT OF FISH AND GAME HEADQUARTERS IN HELENA, MONTANA. I had called ahead and set up an appointment with the guide and outfitters superintendent, Joe Gaab, who was a breath of fresh air after what I had seen in California and especially in Nevada. He actually came across as if he *wanted* to help me get started there and would do whatever he could to get it done. Joe had horses and mules of his own, hunted without a guide, and did his best to travel to Bishop, California, every spring to attend their annual Mule Days Celebration. We talked about the area I was interested in and also asked why Montana didn't allow the use of hounds to hunt bears. He said that some areas of the state had very large populations of black bears, and grizzlies, and the hunter success rate was so high that they could see no reason for allowing the advantage of hounds. In fact, the area where I was interested in hunting had an annual bear kill of 400-500. They had both a spring and fall season and baiting bears was not allowed either, so a hunter simply had to find them on their own, as with hunting deer.

So that's where I was heading for, Lincoln County, the largest county in the state, which was approximately eighty miles each way. It had a number of mountain ranges, including the Cabinet Mountain Wilderness, several rivers, and many lakes, and it also had mountain lions. It all sounded real good, and I wanted to see it. I also liked the idea of living close to the Idaho border where it was legal to hunt bears with hounds, so I was off to Libby, Montana. From Helena, I traveled west through Missoula, and when I approached the Clark Fork River things started to look good, and when I turned north onto Highway 56 and traveled through the Bull River Valley, it really started to shape up. The mountain ranges on each side of the valley were impressive. I set up my camp trailer along the Yaak River and planned to do my scouting from there. It didn't take long before I could see why they had such a large kill rate on black bears.

When bears first come out of hibernation they go after as much grass as they can eat and in that part of Montana the Forest Service had planted clover along the new roads to help prevent erosion, so it seemed as though every bear in the area was feeding alongside the roads that I went on. At times I felt like I was traveling in a national park, because there were bears all over the place, some would barely get out of the road to let you drive by, and there I was with a bunch of bear hounds that I didn't dare let loose. It was April and the spring hunting season was open, and I saw this everywhere I went. When it came to deer, I had never seen so many of them, anywhere. The higher elevations still had a lot of snow, so they were pretty well concentrated in the lower elevations, eating the same thing the bears were, and there were places that I saw hundreds of them all together.

My first thoughts about this place was there had to be lions here, but just how many? I would have to wait until winter to get my answer, and I was definitely going to stay to find out. I needed six months to establish residency before I could get my application in for the Guide License, so by early November I'd be ready. I also needed to either find a place to build a house or get a rental somewhere. I found a small parcel with acreage that was reasonably priced on the east side of Bull Lake just off of Highway 56 and in the middle of what looked to be perfect lion hunting. So I bought it and started building right away.

In the meantime, I started bear hunting in the Northern Panhandle of Idaho just for fun and to get acquainted with the area as I gave my dogs some much needed exercise. I had met with the two local Montana Game Wardens and was glad to see that they were very receptive to my setting up business in their area. I went into Libby to see about getting a building permit for the house and learned that the only permits I needed to build a house was one for electrical and septic, and the septic permit was free. This was quite a welcome surprise after coming from California where a permit was required for just about everything. So I was on my way and needed to get that new house built before the snow started to fly.

The biggest drawback to the move was that I couldn't do any advertising for hunts until I received my Outfitters License, and since the majority of the guided lion hunts were usually made during the summer and fall months, I could be without any hunts until late in the season. But this was okay with me, since I really didn't know much about the lion population there anyway. So I established myself as a Montana resident, passed the test for Outfitters by early November, and was ready for business when the season opened. But as expected, I had no customers scheduled.

1974/75 Season
First day of season

I took the time to see what was available, and on the first day of the season, I caught a good-sized female lion and let her go. Then I called a guy I knew to see if he wanted it, and just as I thought, he did. Two days later I took him out on a hunt, we caught it again, and I was back in business. We got it less than three miles from where I lived, and because of the perfect cover of snow, it was also an easy catch. I would like to point out that before I moved there I had checked with the Montana records for lion kills and found that they were only killing about eighty to a hundred and twenty lions per year. This didn't look too good to me, since places like California and other western states took in quite a few more than this, but I had dismissed it; I thought maybe there were not that many lion hunters here, or maybe just not that many lions, but I wanted to see for myself, and knew I'd get my answers soon enough.

Despite the fact that all my older and most experienced dogs had passed in recent years and I lacked at least one well-trained dog for the younger dogs to look up to, I was somewhat pleased with some of the hunting results so far. To expect a high rate of success as a professional hunting guide, the use of well-trained and hardened dogs is almost always required, especially when it comes to bears. The loss of Flipper at the beginning of 1974 was devastating, so I contacted my very good friend Louis Strawn. When I needed an extra dog, Louis would always loan me at least one, and in some cases, all of his dogs. Louis had a dog named Hammer, that was pretty good, and I liked him a lot. I borrowed him off and on over the past four years on bear hunts, and he would always tough it out with the best of them.

I called Louis, and much to my surprise, he agreed to sell Hammer to me. So in January of 1975, Hammer was on his way to Montana. This really helped when the spring season opened in Idaho, and I started doing better on the bear hunts with his help. By the time the fall season had closed, I was catching about seventy percent of all the bears that my dogs were getting after, and that was more than I actually expected. I had also learned that on the average, most of the bears there were quite a bit smaller than the ones

I was used to seeing in California, but that's ok, they were bears, and there were lots of them.

One thing of special interest was that no matter where I hunted, the smaller ones were usually hardest on the dogs. It wasn't that the bigger ones couldn't be mean and give the very best bear dogs an all-around bad time, but more often than not, the adults that ranged in size between 120 pounds to 200 pounds were more agile, ran the fastest, and could run down and do more damage to the hounds who had the courage to get in close. So, here I am, new to that area, had lost all of my best bear dogs, and was trying to catch these tough little bears in some pretty rough country, with a bunch of young dogs. So it seemed that in many ways I am starting all over again. To help verify my thoughts about the sizes of local bears, I took the hide of the one I had killed in White River in 1973, the one with the white letter "H" to a taxidermist who had a studio alongside the Kootenai River, between the towns of Troy and Libby. He did an excellent job on bear rugs and I wanted to see what he would charge for a full rug mount. This bear hadn't been weighed, but I was pretty good at guessing weights and I estimated it at 300 to 325 pounds, field dressed.

After he rolled out the tanned hide onto the counter to take a look at it, the first thing he said was, "This is not a local bear." He was right, it was killed about 1,200 miles to the south, but I was surprised that he would know this. I asked him how he knew this, and he said it was easy; the size was a dead giveaway. This one was the largest black bear hide that had ever come through his door, and he processed well over one hundred each year. After I hunted in the northern part of Idaho and Montana where I caught hundreds of black bears over a fifteen-year period, I can honestly say that I never saw any in the area that came close to tipping the scales at 300 pounds after they had been field dressed. This had to be due to the limited number of days that the bears were out of hibernation, and the type of food that was available to them. The bears in the Sierra and Southern Cascade Mountain Ranges lived in such a mild climate, and it gives them more time out of their dens, and since California has so many oaks, the bears had a lot of acorns to eat, which surely helped to put on the pounds.

By 1975, I was in need of additional income, and from what I could see; this area of Montana was wide open for building houses. I had just finished building my own house at Bull Lake and there was a couple that lived about a mile south of me who liked what I had done, so we cut a deal to build them a house; I was going to supplement my income as a builder. Much to my surprise, that part of the world was totally different from where I had just come from. The couple was Stan and Chris Tallmadge, and Stan was about my age, worked with his father as a logging contractor, and to say the least, was quite an accomplished hunter. We hit it off right away and in a short time he became a very good friend and hunting partner. His real specialty was elk, but he eventually started coming with me on lion hunts. He knew the area as well as anyone, understood more than most about the animals that lived there, and didn't care how hard it might get following the dogs. Eventually, I started loaning him my dogs to hunt without me and there was one year when Stan was off hunting on his own that he actually ended up catching more lions with my dogs than I did.

1976 was off to a good start. I had taken out a few clients, and then one night I received a phone call from a lion hunter who lived in Libby, which is about twenty miles east of Troy, and beside the Kootenai River. He had lion hounds and hunted only part time, but he did a pretty good job of catching his fair share with what little time he had. He told me that a few days earlier, he had been hunting in the Callahan Creek drainage and found where a very large male lion had crossed the road. It looked to him like it might have had a trap on its left front foot. It was hard to tell for sure just what was going on, because the snow was about a foot deep and a very light powder. Whatever it was, it looked like he was dragging it. The track was fresh and he let his three hounds go after it, and off they went.

The lion had come off the southern slope of Preacher Mountain, and was heading south into Callahan Creek. Where it crossed it was a steep drop of about four hundred feet, and almost straight down. It was late in the afternoon when he did this, and he was hoping for an easy catch. Instead, he lost track of his dogs within minutes, then tried to trail them as best that he could, and as night fell, he still wasn't able to find them. He returned the next day in hopes of finding them, and again the day after that, but no dogs. His job required him to be at work everyday, so he could only look for them after work, and that wasn't working, so he had called to ask for my help. Without any hesitation, I told him that I'd start looking in the morning. I quickly called Stan, who lived only about a half mile from me on Bull Lake Road, told him the story, and asked if he wanted to come along. He immediately said, "What time are we going?" The next morning we headed out to Callahan Creek.

The first thing we wanted to see was where all this all started. There was still quite a bit of snow in the road, which made it easy to find where the tracks of the lion crossed the road, and where the dogs had been turned loose on his trail. We also checked the road to see if there was any sign that the lost dogs might have returned, but there was nothing, no dogs. It was now four days ago when this all started and the weather had warmed up to where the daytime temperatures were well above freezing and the snow on the southern slopes of the mountain had been melting off while at the same time the canyon bottoms and northern slope were now covered with a hard crusted snow. Both of us had plenty of experience in tracking, but if the ground is frozen along with the snow crusted on the top, it will not be easy to find any tracks, and even then they would most likely be too old for the dogs to trail them. This is going to take a joint effort between us, and the dogs to unravel this. If we can find any place where the dogs can get just a whiff of lion scent, then they will know there is a lion in this area. I had five dogs with me, Curley, who just turned five years old and was a Bluetick hound (Curley was the son of Saylor). Curley would be the only one that would be let loose to hunt and try to help us find tracks, while Stan and I would try to find any signs of this lion. Here is a four day old lion trail, which will make a real challenge for anyone, and both Stan and I are going to try and catch it. I had caught lions before where the tracks were close to two days old, but nothing like this one. This was quite the challenge, and we're both game for it. The same can be said for the dogs, as well. This was old school lion hunting. In the meantime, Curley hunted ahead of us while the others would be hooked together, and at our side or follow behind us until conditions improved. If we could find where the lion scent is strong enough for Curley to follow at a decent pace, we will let the others join in to add help, but for now, it was touch and go only.

Starting off, we decided it would be best to not start trailing him from Callahan Creek, and instead we would try to second guess where the lion would most likely head for and see if we can cut his tracks there. Since he was already heading south when he crossed the road at Callahan Creek, we both felt that our best bet would be to try and cut his tracks again by heading further out in that same direction. So, we backtracked ourselves down the Callahan Road, headed south a couple of miles to an old mining road that went up Iron Creek Canyon. We drove up there as far as the snow would allow, and then got out and started walking up the canyon. After we went about a mile up the canyon bottom we found part of what we were looking for. No dogs to be found, but here in front of us is the track of a very large male lion, and this has to be him. It appeared to us that once he dropped into Callahan Creek, he headed up July Creek until he came into the headwaters of Iron Creek and from there he turned east again, and went down the north side of Iron Creek until he got to the old Liberty Mine, which was where we were at. He is definitely larger than most, and he is missing a toe on his left front foot. We could only figure that, if he still had the trap on his foot when these missing dogs caught up with him, it would be next to impossible for him to climb a tree, and then there was a fight on the ground. Somewhere during this fight the trap came off, taking a toe with it, and he killed all three dogs. Then he went on his way.

By now, the day had been slipping away from us, so instead of trying to follow him any further, we decided to call it a day. We had made some progress, but still no sign of the missing lion hounds. Early the next morning, we were back to where we had left off and started following the lion track as best we could. His tracks were now five days old, hard to find and still too old for the dogs to trail by themselves, but with the combined efforts of everyone together, we started making some progress. So far, we gained about two miles on him, which we felt good about, but it looked like we are still days behind him. We followed him out of Iron Creek and onto the northwest side of Copper Mountain where the snow was better for trailing, which helped us to move a little faster, and hopefully he was setting still, and if so, we were closing the gap between the lion and us. Then we ran into an area where there were quite a few deer and they had walked over his tracks to the point that we couldn't find anything, and Curley couldn't smell anything either. So, we're back to second-guessing his movements again. This time, we need to get out ahead of all this, and not miss his tracks along the way. We both thought that a good place to do this was to work our way towards the top of Copper Mountain. If we can find any sign of him up there we could be back in business again.

As soon as we got there, we found one place where he had bedded down for a while, it was on the southwest end of the mountain, and we could now assume that we might be getting closer. There was no sign of him trying to catch or kill anything, even though there were plenty of deer to pick from. We knew that, if this lion was just traveling, we could be in for a very long trip, and doubtful if we could ever catch up to him. This didn't matter though, we continued moving forward and now we are about five miles from where we started the day before, and it still didn't look like the tracks were any fresher here than they were when we first started. From time to time, Curley would pick up the trail, acting like things were getting better, but only for short distances and then it was back to bare ground, and all guesswork again. We had no idea how long it had stayed at this one spot, although my guess was that it had just helped us catch up by, at least one or two days.

We were fortunate that it had not rained or snowed at all during the entire time since he was on Preacher Mountain, and if it started doing that now, it would either cover up or washed out any scent or tracks left behind. Challenging as it was, we were determined that as long as we can continue to follow him, we will not quit. As long as the weather will hold out like this, we felt confident that we're going to catch this guy. We didn't know when or where we might catch him, but we're not stopping until he's been caught.

By now we had given up any hope of finding the three missing dogs, and we were quite sure this lion must have killed them. We continued to move on and it's now becoming late in the afternoon.

After he left his camping spot, he came down off of Copper Mountain, crossed Copper Creek, passed by Grouse Lake on its north side and was now heading up the northeast side of Grouse Mountain. For the first time since we started trailing him, Curley was picking up a steady trail and moving out faster and no longer needed any of our help. I didn't want to chance Curley jumping this lion by himself, so I turned the other four dogs loose to run with him and it's a good thing I did. The further they went the faster they ran. As soon as they reached the top of Grouse Mountain they started down its main ridge heading in an easterly direction. Stan and I were doing our best to stay with them, but they are going so fast now that we couldn't keep up, so we simply headed in the same direction that we last heard them.

After going east for about a half-mile we could look due south into North Fork Creek and we could hear the dogs were running wide open. All five of them. Curley, Sue, Mindy, Bonnie, and Hammer were heading straight for the bottom. This was about 1,500 feet of nothing but a straight down, rugged mountainside. Once they hit the bottom, they crossed over North Fork Creek, went around the east end of Pony Mountain, continued heading south and dropped into the Main Fork of Keeler Creek. As soon as they hit the creek bottom, they immediately started baying with everything they had. To both of us, this didn't sound right, something is wrong. We were expecting to hear them bark treed as soon as they hit the canyon bottom, but that wasn't happening. Instead all we heard was a roar of thunder coming from all five dogs that were now in the creek bottom. Here we had five seasoned hounds, all with booming loud voices, and baying as hard as they could. This couldn't possibly be a lion. If it was a lion, he would surely have gone up a tree by now. This sounded more like they had jumped a bear and the fight was on, only there were no bears out at this time of the year, so whatever it is, it was not up a tree and the dogs were going nuts. It's not running from them any longer, and they are looking right at it. It was easy to tell they have no intention of letting it get away.

While this is going on, we are trying to get to them as fast as possible. They are in an almost jungle of heavy brush, stacked up log jams that included several beaver dams, all covered with ice and snow, and these dogs are right in the middle of it. We could hardly see anything over twenty feet away and somewhere in there, there are five hounds going wild over something.

The dogs kept putting on the pressure as best they could and after about twenty minutes of this, they broke and started to run again. And run they did, only this time they were heading up the main fork of Keeler Creek. They only went about one-half mile up then they turned to the north and headed straight up the south side of Pony Mountain. They were too far away from us to see what they were after, but we could tell that they were still looking right at it, and still baying just as hard as they could. Then when they were about half way to the top, they all stopped for a brief moment. The thundering roar of the dogs ceased, then one dog after another, they all started to bark again, only this time they were barking treed. They are only about one quarter mile from us now, and the mountain side that they are at is about as straight up as it can get, but who cares, this thing is up a tree. Now we are going to see what this is all about. I was a little ahead of Stan, and about half way to them when I could see him. There he is! A big Tom lion, about twenty feet up a Douglas fir tree, with all five dogs treeing under it. After a brief stop, I started climbing again, but this time he sees me coming, and he immediately starts to show sign of uneasiness and as soon as I get within twenty feet of him, he jumps out of the tree and is heading back down from where he had just come from only minutes before. As the dogs and the lion were running back towards Keeler Creek, they almost ran over Stan, who was loving every minute of this. This time, it was quick, he ran only about six hundred-feet down the mountainside and up another tree. There's just too many dogs for him to take them on and he knows it. He is big, definitely larger than most, and he has to be the one we were after for the last two days. This time, Stan arrived at the tree ahead of me, looked back at me to see where I was, and at that same time, the lion looked like he was going to jump again. We've had enough of this! Stan takes a quick look towards me, and I signal for him to take it out, and with one quick shot from Stan's Ruger .22 mag., and it was over.

Stan Tallmadge
Hammer on the left, and Curley with his head tucked under Stan's left arm.

The dogs were tired, we were tired, and no one got hurt. We could finally take a closer look to see just what we had. We looked him over and found that he was missing one toe on his left front foot just as we had expected. He also had broken both upper and lower canine teeth on his left side. They were all recent injuries and we were certain that he had been caught in a trap when he crossed Callahan Road. He had probably broken his teeth biting the trap, got it off but lost a toe, and killed all the dogs. We opened up his stomach and found it completely empty, so he had not eaten for some time. Other than all this, he was in excellent condition.

We packed him out and loaded him into our truck and weighed him once we got him home; he weighed 167 pounds. There was no question about it, this old guy was tough and I honestly believed that if we had fewer than five tough well-trained hounds after him at the same time, the outcome could have been the same for them, as it was for the other unfortunate hounds. Stan kept the hide, which he made into an impressive wall rug, and to this day, I still have his skull.

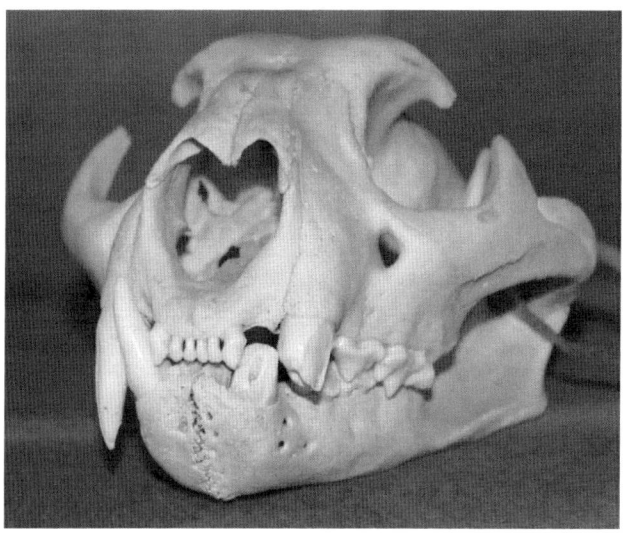

I suppose we could name him 3-toes. As large as he was, he didn't qualify for the 15" skull minimum required for the Boone & Crockett record book? He was close, but just shy by 1/8". That's ok though, he was definitely worth keeping.

By the end of my second year in Montana, I had developed a good relationship with the local Fish and Game Wardens, and people had regularly started to call upon me to build houses. Things were working very well. I could work during the off seasons and then when the winter weather turned to snow, which was almost every day, I could do my lion hunting. As for the bear guiding hunts, I was out of the business. I could still go to Idaho where it was legal to hunt bear with dogs, which I was now doing just for fun; but there was no killing, we just treed them and then let them go, unharmed, and I really enjoyed doing that. I met up with another dog hunter who lived in Naples, Idaho, who had a couple of hounds, and although he didn't care much for lion hunting, he really liked chasing bears. Elmer Nichols was rough around the edges, to say the least. A logger by trade, he took a bath once every Saturday night, whether he needed it or not and had a bunch of kids. Best part was he didn't cuss much, was basically honest and his dogs were fairly good. We ended up being good friends and hunting partners.

I also became friends with one of Montana's Fish and Game Wildlife biologists who lived in Libby. Jerry was originally from California and about my age. We started spending time together as friends, and we also shared similar interest in the population and preservation of the Montana mountain lions. As I recall, it was during one of our hunts together that the discussion turned to mountain lion research. Jerry was new to this and he had a genuine interest in learning as much as possible, and he asked if I would be interested in joining him in proposing a mountain lion research project to the higher-ups in the Game Department. I was all for it. By that time I had been hunting lions and bears with my dogs for about fifteen years and loved the hunts, but was getting tired of all the killing.

Is that lion alive? You bet she is! This is Stan with our number 2 lion. We caught her on the North fork of Bull River, put on a #2 collar, weighed, and tattooed her just as she was about to come out of the tranquilizer. We wanted to take a photo that was just a little different, so here it is! Within 1 minute after setting her down, she was gone and never seen again.

I had witnessed firsthand the lion population in many areas reduced down to almost nothing from what once was a healthy population. In my opinion, that part of Montana should have had more lions in it than it appeared to have. So on January 1, 1976, I was given the authority to live-capture, tattoo, weigh, and place a rope collar on as many lions as I could catch. The number one problem was that I would be mixing paying hunters who wanted to kill the same lions that I was wanting to use in the newly developed research program. It was easy to see that this wasn't going to work, so I quit guiding all together. I kept my dogs and hunted them as often as I wanted, mostly by myself, or occasionally with friends, and after treeing a bear or lion, we would leash up the dogs, congratulate them for what they had just done and walk away, letting the animals go free.

The lion research was totally volunteer and the only thing that Fish and Game provided was the drugs, some paperwork, self-stamped envelopes addressed to their headquarters, and the numbered collars. The rest was up to us, the volunteers with the dogs. I had my own tranquilizer gun and miscellaneous equipment that I had used for live-captures when I was in California. I knew how to use it all quite well and the only problem that I could see was that, unlike other areas where I had hunted before, every single tree that these lions in Montana went up were very tall. Many of the lions would climb forty feet or more when they were treed. Nevada, California, and Utah had similar trees, but they also had pinyon, juniper, oaks, and an assortment of other trees that were more accommodating when it came to live-capturing a lion. I preferred these much better when it came to treed lions who would often perch on a branch much closer to the ground and when they were hit with the tranquilizer they didn't have such a long fall. I knew from experience that it was best for lions to not hit the ground completely unconscious, especially if they fell from above twenty feet and it was a flat landing. By the thirteenth of January, I had collared my first lion for the State Fish and Game Department and I still had some guiding to do. But this would be my last season as a guide, and the next season I could completely concentrate on the research program.

Around this same time, there was a new copper mine going in around the Bull Lake area and the government required an environmental impact statement to assess the impact on the area. They then sent Gail, a Fish and Game biologist, to conduct the study. I met with her and she asked if she could accompany me on some of my hunts. She was in good physical shape and could hold her own in some of the toughest conditions. One day, the two of us, along with Gerry, the local biologist, treed an orphaned lion kitten, and because of its size, we couldn't use a tranquilizer gun. It had gone only about twenty feet up a really bushy Douglas fir, so we attached a hypodermic syringe to a pole and Gerry climbed to within reach and carefully poked it in the hip with just enough drug to put it asleep. He then tied a rope to its back leg and lowered it down to where Gail and I could take ahold of it and put it into a burlap sack. This kitten was the lone survivor of a mother lion that was killed by another hunter. We checked the area where he had put his dogs after them and could see that she had three kittens with her. Besides the one that we caught alive, we were only able to locate one other, and it was dead. Because of their size and age, I could only assume that the other one had died as well.

We took the kitten, a female of about ten pounds, to the Fish and Game headquarters in Libby, where she was fed road-killed deer for about six months. Then she was fitted with a radio collar and returned to the Cabinet Mountain Wilderness. I was quite concerned about the lion being turned loose so young, and not being able to fend for herself, but about two months later I flew with the Game Department over that area and sure enough, she was still alive, and we estimated that she was about nine months old by that point. They located her again a short time later, then lost all radio contact, and that was the last anyone ever saw of her.

Back when I was living in Glennville, I had kept a young male, who was about the same size as this female kitten, however, his eyes had opened, just like hers were by the time he was caught. I had always been told that if they were captured after their eyes were open they could not be trained as pets. That seemed to be true, because as long as I had him, I needed to wear heavy-duty welder gloves just to pick him up. This little female was still slightly sedated when we caught her, therefore I was able to hold her with my bare hands.

I had become very satisfied with doing this kind of work instead of guiding hunts. Not that I ever regretted guiding, but I needed a change from what I was doing, and I want to point out that over the years of guiding I had become friends with many of my hunters, and most of them were thankful for the animals they killed while hunting with me, and that made it all worthwhile. The truth is, the more I hunted, the greater the respect I gained for these animals. But, the time had come for me to move on to something a little different, and I felt that doing this would give me an opportunity to pay back a little something to the animals that I had enjoyed hunting so much.

Compared to many other places that I had hunted, Montana turned out to be by far the easiest place to catch lions. Because of this, I think that I started to lose interest in hunting them, and I could suddenly see a need for some control. Instead of killing them, or simply treeing them and then letting them go, I wanted to help in some way to make sure that there would always be a balanced population and I felt that Montana Fish and Game was the answer. Then, one day while I was talking with Ken, who was the director of the Mountain Lion Research Team, he asked me why I wasn't tagging more lions. I told him that most of the lions I had caught in the areas where I hunted would tree in Douglass fir or Larch trees, and usually so high up that I didn't feel comfortable with darting them with a tranquilizer, just to watch them fall, unconscious, some thirty or even forty feet, and then hit the ground. I had seen several lions injured and killed by falling only half that distance, so I would simply let them go, and document them as treed.

Much to my surprise, he told me to dart them anyway, and if they died in a fall, it would be okay. It surprised me to hear that he felt that way. So I asked him what was being done with all the information that myself, and others who were involved were sending to him? This answer came to me as no surprise when he said: "Nothing". It was simply placed in a "confidential file" in his office at the Fish and Game Wildlife Laboratory, MSU, Bozeman, Montana. So then I asked him, "Then, if nothing is being done with this information, why we are we doing this?" I wasn't surprised by the next answer, in fact I had heard this said before when I was in California. He told me that, "This was all being done in an effort to convince the general public into believing that the Game Department was doing everything possible to properly manage the lion population." "Really," I said. "Well, that's not why I'm doing this!" And it all reminded me of the time in California when the two Fish and Game wardens tried to fool me into believing they were going to live transport a trouble-making bear to another location, all the while never having any intention of it surviving the process

By now, I was getting a new picture of what was really going on, and I had learned that it wasn't the animals that needed to be managed as much as it was some people, and that included some of them that were put in places of both law enforcement and game management. The question was, who could be trusted to do *this*? The Asarco Mining study had almost been completed by then and Gail needed a little more information to finish her Environmental Impact Statement in the Bull Lake area. So she asked if she could use my confidential information about the lions to go along with her other observations. I gave her permission, PROVIDING, none of this information would be made public. She agreed and said she understood the importance of confidentially. By now I had known her for quite some time, and I trusted her to do only that which was right. This all took place during the winter of 1976-77.

In late spring of 1977, she stopped by my home and told me that she had completed her work here and would be leaving the area. Before leaving she wanted to give me copies of her work. It came in the form of two volumes titled, *Troy Project, Asarco Inc., Lincoln County, Montana*. On pages 190 -191 of Volume 1, was a written report of my private and confidential Mountain Lion Study, which started off with, "Mountain Lion observations and signs recorded from 1974 (this was incorrect, it was actually 1975) through spring of 1977" on a study that was actually conducted by me. It went on to say, "Forty-two of the sixty-seven lion observations were provided by Ed Vance, hounds-man, and cooperator in the Montana Department of Fish and Game Lion marking program." Then on page 192 there was a photocopy of my map showing the exact location of everything that I had provided the Fish and Game over the past two seasons. Upon receiving these books I asked Gail, "Where will these books be placed?" and her answer was hard to believe. She went on to explain that they would be placed in every library, Fish and Game office, school, and National Forest Building throughout the state. I was sure she had no idea of what she had just done, but she may as well have published this information in many of the nation's leading hunting magazines. This area had no restrictions on lion hunting and was wide open to hunt for all. She had opened the floodgates.

Lion #3. This male lion was darted while being about 35 feet up in a Douglass Fir tree. Instead of coming out on his own, he passed out. Then after being hung up by one back leg, he slid into a straight up and down position. Then fell head first to the ground below. Had it not been for the ground being on a slope and covered with about one foot of snow, he would have been killed by the fall.

He was tranquilized with a drug known as sernylan, which was great for cats except it didn't wear off very fast. Gerry and I stayed with him for about 6 hours making sure that he would be alright. The last thing that we dared to do was leave him to where he could not defend himself. If left that way, and found by birds, such as ravens and crows they would most likely start in by pecking out his eyes while he laid there. Strange as it may sound, both Gerry and I actually straddled and rubbed both his body and head while he was waking up. In fact I was rubbing his head and ears only minutes before taking this photo, he actually acted like he was enjoying it.

I returned the following day to check on him. I left my dogs in the truck and found where we left him. From there he walked only about one quarter mile and then bedded down. He stayed there until he saw me coming, and then got up and started walking up hill, turning around about every one hundred feet to see what I was doing. I saw no blood or any thing that made me feel like he was injured, so I turned around and left him.I could only assume that he was okay, so I left him be, and was never seen again. Question now is, did he really survive the fall? I have no idea, but I do know that doing this can be dangerous.

The following winter the Bull River Drainage, as well as surrounding areas were overrun with hound hunters. Hound hunters showed up from all of the surrounding states and as far away as Texas, and Florida. Because of this, I resigned my position, sold all of my live-capture equipment to my friend Gerry, and I quit hunting lions altogether. Everything that I had been trying to accomplish had been inadvertently desecrated. The people I trusted had no accountability for their actions and the impact on the wildlife. But I kept my dogs and continued to hunt them, but only for bears. I continued to hunt this way for another seven years and only for sport. I did no guiding and no killing at all. We would simply run and tree the bears, and then let them go to maybe run again another day. Then one morning when the alarm went off at about 3 AM, I asked myself as I was getting out of bed, "Why am I doing this?" I had been hunting with my dogs for over twenty-five years, and back in California I had hunted them nonstop, every month of the year. In Montana, my dogs would now be laid up for about five to six months at a time while we waited for the bears to come out of hibernation, and I couldn't get accustomed to seeing them living like this. I guess I must have been spoiled, but this just was not my way of hunting, or treating my dogs.

There had been many changes in the laws since I had started hunting, and Idaho was no exception. As early as 1980, the use of dogs to hunt for bear in the panhandle area was on the chopping block. It wasn't because there weren't enough bears in those areas, it was because the illegal, immoral, and unethical sale of bear gallbladders had become very popular with some hound hunters and it had gone out of control. To make things worse, some of these "hunters" would travel in large numbers. I had seen as many as five to seven truckloads full of thirty or more hounds come in to hunt—if you want to call that hunting. These outlaw hunters would all hunt together in a mob, throwing as many dogs as they could get together, all after one bear in an attempt to kill as many bears as they could. In the eyes of the general public and those who hunted with hounds in a truly sporting manner, this did not look good. It would only be a matter of time before the

State Game Department would close the area off to using hounds to hunt for bears. This was not the way that most of the hound hunters behaved, but because of this, they would all pay the price. I had seen something like this before, back in California, and it was hard to believe it was happening again, in Idaho. It seemed like no one was able to stop this cycle, once it had started.

Chapter 18

BEAR HUNTING IN IDAHO

Back when I was still new to the game of bear hunting with hounds, my friend Willis Butolph told me the difference between good and bad bear dogs. He simply put it like this, *"If you can't catch bears with three to four dogs, you don't need more, you just need new ones,"* and in time, I learned that he was right. I had my share of good to better than-good hounds, lost most of them to just about everything imaginable, and it was a hard pill to swallow with the loss of each and every one of them. The good ones were hard to find and when I had them, they actually became my best friends, partners, and family. I had hunted professionally in four western states, and hunted for fun with my dogs in an additional five states. I met and hunted with a few outstanding lion and bear hunters, some of whom were also professional hunters, and others who just hunted because they enjoyed hunting with hounds. Over the years, I caught more than enough animals to satisfy myself, but to me it was really more about the dogs than what we were hunting. It was about raising, training, and watching a young hound as it develops into something special, and with the hopes of seeing something of excellence somewhere along the way. I never thought that those who hunted with a mob of hounds had any of this in mind. I may have been spoiled, but as times changed and there were more hunters and more laws, my interest in the sport started dropping like a rock. It was easy to see that I was now only doing this for my dogs, which I cared for with a passion, and nothing else.

Then, early one morning as I was heading for one of my favorite places to bear hunt and I saw four lions standing in the road all together. It was just about to break daylight and a friend who was with me wanted to see if the dogs would try and tree them. It had been several years since any of these dogs had hunted for lions and I was interested to see what would happen. So we dropped the tailgate of the pickup truck and expected to see all of my dogs run after them, but nothing happened; they acted as though there was nothing there. I had to admit, that even I was surprised. Every one of my dogs was now totally tuned into running bears only. I guess you could say that I couldn't catch a lion now if my life depended on it, and that was just fine with me.

Back when it was still my favorite thing to do, it was always the most satisfying to go on a long and difficult hunt that took both hounds and hunter working together over rough terrain and trying conditions until we ended with a treed lion. Montana, like many other northwestern states have always been known for their winter snows which gave the hunters an advantage of having a blanket of white where tracks stood out; this definitely simplified finding and even catching them. At the same time California's heavily brush covered Mountains and bare ground trailing conditions of the southern Los Padres National Forest were by far the toughest to find, trail, and tree anything. Everywhere else that I hunted fell somewhere between these two degrees of difficulty. It actually required a different type of hunter and better-trained dogs to be successful in the more rugged areas, and even though one could catch many more lions in the snow areas, I missed the bare ground lion and bobcat hunting.

Eventually, I had successfully hunted my dogs in just about every type of terrain and climate in the lower forty-eight states, that went from the swamps of Mississippi and Alabama, cornfields and hill country of Arkansas, Oklahoma and Missouri, dry and arid mountains of Southern

California coastal ranges, Southern Sierras, Cascades and Coast ranges of Northern California, high deserts and mountain ranges of Nevada, and in several areas of the Rocky Mountains in Utah, Idaho and Montana. Two of my dogs, Bo and Saylor made it to all of these States except for Idaho and Montana.

By the spring of 1988, I was down to only three very well trained Bluetick hounds that would usually catch more than ninety percent of the bears that they got after.

But now, my dogs had not hunted since the fall of the previous year. They wanted to get out there and they deserved something better than the life I had to offer. I was missing the days when I hunted in the Greenhorn Mountains of California, and the times when I could hunt twelve months out of the year. I knew that those days were gone.

Then late one afternoon as I went out to feed, I found Mandy, who was only six years old, curled up in her dog house, she had died from something unknown. After burying her, I made a phone call that I never thought I'd make. I got in touch with Bill Reynolds, a close friend who had hunted with me off and on for several years. At the time, I was down to only two dogs, Spud and Sugar. They were both close to eight years old and had treed close to three hundred bears. They had never seen a bear killed, much less heard a gun go off, which I thought was a perfect example of sport hunting with hounds. Bill practiced and believed in this way of hunting as well, and I wished that every hound hunter felt the way we did. He loved to hunt with the hounds, and knowing he would take good care of them, I offered to give him Spud and Sugar, and everything that went with them.

After that, I hunted only one time, about eight years later, in Susanville, California with my old friend, Jim Bridges, who has since passed away. Jim was as good as they got when it came to bear hunters, and always had exceptionally good hounds. We caught one bear on that hunt, and as usual, we let it go to run another day. Since then, I have been asked many times; if given the chance, would I do this all over again? My answer has always been the same: *yes*. I would do it in a heartbeat, but only if I could roll back time. I knew it was over.

Now all that's left are the memories.

1967
Bo and Saylor
***Just the two of them, at the head waters of
Squaw Creek, Shasta County, California***

PART II

Chapter 19

BITS & PIECES

Curley

Here is Curley with a bear he treed close to the Moyie River in Northern Idaho. This was the first time Curley had treed a bear all by himself. The dog in the background is his sister Sue.

The following series of photos like these are not that easy to get, or for that matter, it is not every day that something like this happens. This is Curley trying to catch a bear as it was jumping out of a tree. The other dogs are Mindy and Bonnie, left to right. Sue is also there, but we can't see her just yet.

Photo #1

Photo #2

These photo's were taken with a Nikon II camera with a motor drive set at 5 frames per second. Total time for all three photo's amounted to just over ½ second; you can see Curley has flipped completely over, and is heading to the ground while the others are attempting to get a mouthful.

Photo #3

That did it! Curley is on the far right, and he has come down with a crash landing, Mindy has a mouth full. Sue in the background and Bonnie, the Redtick are trying their best to get ahold of the Bear.

All four of these dogs were related. Their mother was a Bluetick we called Fannie, I got her from a man in Mississippi. She was all Vaughn bred. The Father to the Blueticks was Saylor and Bo was the Father to the Redtick, Bonnie.

Unfortunately for Curley, when he landed as shown in photo #3 he injured his ear which was a problem that he endured for the rest of his life.

Photo #4

This time the Bear hit the ground running but he didn't go very far and decides to take a stand on the ground. Curley is the Bluetick in front of me with Mindy baying it on the right. Within seconds of taking this photo, the bear ran Curley down, then standing on top of him, and holding him down with it's back feet, it started pounding and clawing on his side with it's front feet attempting to cave in his ribs, or tear a hole into his side. At the same time, Sue, Bonnie, and Mindy got all over the bear, distracting it enough where Curley got out from under it. Then the bear broke away, ran only a short distance and bayed up again giving myself and hunting partner, Elmer enough time to gathered up the dogs and let this guy go on his way. Surprisingly as it was, there were no injuries to any of these dogs, however if it wasn't for Curley's three sisters with him, I'm sure this would have been his last hunt. As usual, neither Elmer nor I had a gun with us on this hunt, and it's probably just as well that we didn't.

Curley eventually became my main dog, but getting him there wasn't easy, and I was surprised when he finally proved himself capable. As a young dog he thought that everything that left a trail was okay for him to run, and I mean everything. I couldn't even come close to guessing how many porcupines he tried to kill, or over time, how many porcupine quills he had stuck in, and pulled out of him. I do remember one time in particular when he had over 300 removed all at one time. Eventually, he got over doing that, and the same held true with him chasing everything except for lions and bears. He turned out to be a better than average bear and lion dog, that was for sure, and you can see by these photos that he wasn't afraid of anything. He never would have been a match for his father, Saylor or a few of the others that I had when I lived in California, but I hunted him differently than I did those others. He was as hard-headed as they get, which made training him to do what I wanted and breaking him from doing what he wanted wasn't easy, but he eventually learned that the consequences for not obeying wasn't worth it, and from then on, he did just fine. He was a character, and it seemed as though everyone that knew him, loved him. I received only one female pup that he sired, Dolly. By the time Dolly had reached the age of 2, she was showing to have the same qualities of her grand father Saylor. Unfortunately she died from an accident at the age of only 3 years old.

Curley died from cancer at the age of only seven.

Howard Bilton

1904 – 1961

1961

Memorial Award presented to

California State Lion Hunter

Howard Bilton

This plaque can to be seen by all at the Kern River Park, Kernville, California

Here's a guy that seemed to have slipped under the radar in the circle of professional lion hunters. Howard lived in the Southern Sierras of Tulare and Kern Counties and was one of the fulltime lion hunters employed by State of California during the bounty days. I had heard a little about Howard before moving to Glennville and knowing that he had lived there at one time, I thought it would be good to learn as much about him as possible. My first move was to find out just how many lions he had actually caught, so in June of 1967, I wrote to the State Fish and Game Department and asked if I could see the record of how many lions he bountied. While I was at it, I included the names of a few other, better-known lion hunters.

Howard Bilton
Actual date and location is unknown

Much to my surprise I learned that the State Fish and Game Department did not keep individual kill records prior to January 1, 1951, nor after September 30, 1963, which was when the bounty in this state was discontinued. It was somewhat of a surprise to learn the number of actual documented kills that were reported, instead of the usual hearsay. As compared to other parts of the West, such as Utah, Nevada, and Arizona, the totals taken by some of these hunters would be considered small, but when you know something about each area where these hunters were hunting, the big difference was clear. What I mean is, when you take into account that all lion country is not the same, and the statistics for each area will no doubt be different. You must consider the difficulty or ease of access, how many lions are actually there, and what the trailing conditions are, bare ground or snow. They all add up, and when you consider that a large number of lions caught in California were caught on dry ground, then the difference in numbers is easy to understand. Over the years, I have heard of how many lions that were supposedly killed by certain hunters and the claims ranged from reasonable to the impossible.

During the winter of 1967, I stopped in to see Wiley Carroll at his home in Ely, Nevada. Wiley seemed to be a straight forward guy and also very believable. It was widely accepted that he caught as many lions as anyone, and when I asked him if he knew how many he had killed, he said it was just a little under five hundred, give or take a few, with killing sixty of them in one year, and catching as many as six in one day. In this latter case, he told me that there were two females and four kittens, all traveling together. He went on the explain that unlike a trophy hunt, the government wanted every lion killed, regardless of age or size, so these numbers included all of them. He also told me that the way this all happened was, an interstate truck driver saw them crossing highway 50 late at night, and when he arrived in Ely he told this to a gas station attendant, who called Wiley, and told him exactly where he saw them and from there the race was on. Wiley said that they all went up the same tree together, and one by one they all died there.

When I asked if he had to do it over again, could it be done now, and his answer was no, there just weren't enough lions out there anymore. I got the same answer from Willis Butolph who at that time was right behind Wiley on documented lions killed. Willis' record kill for one year was forty-four. In California, Jay Bruce looks to hold the record of 669 documented lion kills. Jay Bruce and Charley Ledshaw were the first to be hired by the state as lion hunters. In addition to their wages, they also received payment for the use of their vehicle, dogs, horse, (if they had one), and the bounty money for each lion they killed. This was also provided to those who were employed by the government, such as Willis Butolph and Wiley Carroll.

There seems to be no question about Bruce's record but there is a little controversy on the number of lions that Ledshaw had killed, as well as some others. I have read reports for Charlie Ledshaw kills ranged somewhere between from 254-308, but whatever it is, he is accepted to be second in line behind Jay Bruce, for highest number of lions bountied in California.. There was a study conducted by the *Wildlife Extension, U.C. Davis, Biological Status of Mountain Lions in California.* In this study, they claim that the combined kills of Bruce and Ledshaw amounted to more kills than the next ten lion hunters. That included both government, state, and private hunters combined. Jay Bruce hunted from 1914 to 1947, which was when he retired, giving him an average of twenty plus lions per year, and in 1927 he killed forty-three. I never was able to find when Charley Ledshaw was first hired, but he retired at about the same time as Bruce. It is interesting to note that no one after Bruce could match his numbers, and from there the average number of kills per hunter started to plummet.

So what does all this mean? Was Bruce that much better than all the rest? Or were there simply more lions back then? Don't get me wrong here, Jay Bruce was probably as good as any that ever hunted for lions, but it looks like he had an edge on others that followed him. According to state records, there were far more lions bountied in the earlier years than there were in the final years. As an example, there were 482 lions bountied in 1908 and as time went on and the number of lion hunters increased, the kills declined, and in 1962 there were 114 bountied, and 105 in 1963. That alone would indicate that their population had been reduced. I was never able to find out when Howard Bilton or Charley Ledshaw had started their career as a lion hunter. However, I did find out that from 1951 and until he died in 1961, Howard had killed 114 lions. Not wanting to count the year Howard died, that would have given him an average of about thirteen lions per year. Then there was one of the better-known California Lion hunters, Steve Matthes who killed 138 in his last twelve years. As for the total lions killed by some of these hunters who hunted prior to 1951 who knows. Whatever the numbers are, I am sure that in their earlier years they had higher averages than later on. Also, I want to point out that none of these early lion hunters had the advantage of using 4X4 quads and trucks with all the bells and whistles, logging roads cut all over the lion country, snow mobiles, shocking collars to help train dogs, GPS devices used to follow their dogs, walkie-talkies, and cell phones, to keep in touch with hunting partners, etc. For the most part they did everything alone. On the other hand, the state and government hunters did have the help from the Fish and Game and the public who notified them of problem lions. When this happened they were given the exact locations of where to find them. This was usually on private land that was not open to anyone except them. All of which made everything easier. My experience in hunting for lions, proved over and over again, that finding a lions trail that is fresh enough for the dogs to follow was the hardest part of catching a them, and once found it was usually all up to the dogs from that point on.

    As the years have gone by, I also found that when I first started hunting, most people thought differently about hunting for lions then, and equally so for the men that hunted them. Today it is different. Regardless, I know from my own experience that these men had to be tough and were usually admired and respected by most and were made welcome for ridding the land of a predator that could wreak havoc on just about anything. As you can see above, in 1961, the same year that Howard died, there was an award placed in his honor at the Kern River county park in Kernville, California. That plaque remains there today. When I moved into the same area where Howard had lived and hunted, I was surprised to learn that the older hound hunters that hunted there didn't seem to know much about him, and then there were those who had never heard of him.

Eastern California Bounty Hunter Charlie Tant

Pictures like this one from 1957 in Inyo County didn't sit well with many "so called" animal rights activists and protectors of wild life. It shows Charlie Tant, who was one of the better known lion hunters in California. He was born in Texas at the turn of the century and as a youngster he hunted with the legendary lion and bear hunter, Ben Lilly. Charlie eventually lived a life very much like Ben Lilly, which was as simple and as rough as it could get. It was just Charley with his Walker Hounds always by his side. He was a true bounty hunter who lived on the bounty money from the lions he killed and the hides he sold, which wasn't much and gave him little to nothing to live on. He had no 4x4 pick-up truck, travel trailer, or house to go home to, and no horses or mules to ride. He simply followed his dogs step-by-step without any modern conveniences from start to finish, and other than Ben Lilly, I have never known of anyone else to have spent a lifetime hunting this way. It's doubtful that anyone knows for sure just how many lions he caught in his lifetime, but whatever it was, it was enough to support himself and his dogs.

Another Charlie Tant photo (unknown year) and believed to be somewhere in the Course Gold area of California. It shows approximately ten lion hides, along with Charlie and his hounds. He collected a bounty of only twenty dollars in the early years, and then in 1945 the bounty was bumped up to fifty dollars for males and sixty for the females. In addition to the bounty money, he could sell the hides to either fur buyers or private parties.

Charlie Tant died in 1977, at the age of seventy-eight and he is buried in Lone Pine, California. His grave is marked by a simple head stone with this inscription:

Charlie Tant – Lion Hunter. 1899 – 1977.

Sometimes that's all you need to say.

Bergin Riddle & Ted Hasty

1960 photo was taken at Camp Schiedeck in Ventura County.

Bergin Riddle and Ted Hasty, both very successful and well-known hunters in that area.

Ventura and Santa Barbara Counties in California have never been considered by most modern-day hunters as great places to go to hunt for either lion or bears. But there was a time when those who were tough enough or good enough to take on the challenge could find hunting there worthwhile. In fact, this area was at one time a favorite for both Charley Tant and Jay Bruce. I think it would be safe to say that almost a hundred percent of all successful hunts in that area were conducted on foot and on bare ground, with dry and hot conditions and in deep canyons that are covered with chaparral and Manzanita so thick that crawling through, under, or even on top of it was more a rule than an exception. Santa Barbara County, as small as it is, accounted for 499 lion bounties and I can assure you that not many were easily caught.

The lions in that region were not the largest of the species, but aside from that, they were as difficult to catch as any place that I know. When it came to bears, there weren't nearly as many in those mountains as in many other places, but what they lacked in numbers they seemed to make up for in size. In 1990 there was a bear killed in Ventura county that placed fifth in the Boon and Crockett record book with a skull measurement of 22 13/16 inches.

1964

Two day hunt at the forks of Cedar and Alder Creeks in the Greenhorn Mountains of

Kern County

Here's a photo of the Riddle brothers and me at Alder Creek Campground in Sequoia National Forest, with Bergin on the left and Roy in the center. Both were Government trappers and occasional guides. The dogs are Bo, Charlie, and Rounder in front and Lead and Red in back.

This shows one raccoon, one bobcat and one female lion. All caught on bare ground and within two days and two miles of where we were standing.

1967

Frog Meadows & Tobias Creek area in the Greenhorns

This is me in the Tobias and Frog Meadows area of Sequoia National Forest in 1967. Because of the many steep and deep canyons in the Greenhorn Mountains I wasn't able to use my horse as much as I could in places such as Nevada and Utah. Sure, I could ride most of the trails there as I looked for tracks, but lions only used those trails for very short distances, and once they got off them, the horse could become more of a burden than a help, and it was all on foot from there.

My horse was always there when I needed him and he could be trusted to do anything I required. Carrying lions dead or alive, was no problem, it didn't bother him. Another plus was that I could carry him in the back of my pickup truck. I had my friend Russ Larsen, who lived in Sugarloaf Village weld together the combination horse and dog rack that is shown here in the back of my truck. No ramp was needed; I just parked on level ground, dropped the tailgate, opened the swing door, and my horse jumped right in. Yes, I named him "Horse". When I wanted him out, he pulled his front hooves back to his back hooves and kicked himself out backwards. Either way, it took less than a minute. He did that as gracefully as you can image. Without a trailer it was very easy and quick to get around on the dirt roads, or anywhere I needed to take him. When I didn't need him, I sometimes loaned him out to a couple of select friends. He wouldn't win any beauty contests, but he definitely shinned as a mountain horse. Then one day in the early hours of a Sunday summer morning while he was standing with some other horses in a horse corral at Panorama Heights, someone shot him with a high powered rifle and killed him. The corral was where the fire station now sits, far enough away from the lodge and other cabins where no one was able to see who did it.

It was such a senseless and puzzling situation. I immediately contacted the local Tulare County Deputy Sheriff. The following day he came to where I had moved his body. I learned that he had been shot from the behind, with the bullet entering just a little to the left side of his tail, and he had actually lived for about eight hours after he was shot. The deputy sheriff told me that the day before he had been called into the area and there were three young men shooting around some of the cabins. He took down their names and the serial numbers of their three guns, one of which was an Army surplus WWII bolt action rifle that was chambered for .303 British military ammunition. This same person was shooting, .303 full metal jacket ammunition in his rifle. The deputy said that in his opinion, this was the gun that killed my horse, but I stood little to no chance of getting anywhere with an arrest and conviction. I asked why, and he said that they were all from the Los Angeles area and the one with the .303 was the grandson of a very famous celebrity who at that time was worth billions of dollars. I could only assume that the deputy knew what he was talking about, but I didn't care how much his grandfather was worth, I wanted him caught. We performed a sort of autopsy by opening up my horse in hopes of locating the bullet. We started at the entry area and followed the holes as the bullet passed through his intestines without expanding, which indicated that it was military jacketed. Then, as the wound passed through the lung area, the bullet seemed to disappear. By then, we were totally convinced as to who did it, but could never prove it for sure. Without the fatal bullet never being found the investigation came to an end. Losses like that are usually hard, but in this case, he was so special that he was impossible for me to replace.

A Bear Killed Douglas Fir Trees

Because of damage like this to young Douglas fir trees in the Northwest, bears in some of those areas were killed by the thousands. What they were after here is the cambium layer, which grows between the outer bark and the core or wooded part of the tree. Apparently, this was something that they liked enough to strip off the outer bark, which kills the tree by girdling it. This photo was taken in the Bull Lake area of Montana.

Over the years I guided and hunted with many bowhunters for both lions and bears, and from just about all walks of life. Most Bowhunters just liked hunting only with a bow and arrow, it was their way of doing things. Then there were those who took a more serious approach to it. There were even a few that became quite well known. Below is Bob Gulman, an avid archery hunter, who lived in Southern California, and fell into the group of better known Bowhunters. We caught this lion just below Bohna Peak in Sequoia National Forest. Bob's wife Betty was also well known in the archery circles.

Bob Gulman in the saddle with my horse, and a lion he killed while hunting with me.

1972

Late fall on the Kern Plateau

Bear hunting wasn't just for the guys, and neither was it by using a bow and arrow. Here with well-known archery hunter, author and photographer, Midge Dandridge. The dogs with her are Flipper and Sue. Midge enjoyed this type of hunting so much that she took two bears while hunting together with me.

1968

Bear in Panorama Heights with screenwriter Bill Keys

This bear was taken not far from Panorama Heights in the Sequoia National Forest. This hunter was a well-known screenwriter, William Keys, who at the time, had a cabin in Panorama Park. Bill wrote movies and TV scripts, including several episodes of the western T.V. series, Gunsmoke. I met Bill at the Panorama Heights Resort in 1967. He told me that he lived in the Hollywood area, but he would come to his cabin at Panorama Park and this was where he felt he could do his best writing, especially when writing a western. I took Bill with me on several occasions, catching both bears and one very large lion that we let go in the Whiter River canyon.

Although this bear was never weighed, both Gary and I estimated it to be somewhere between 220 to 250 pounds field dressed. I also believe it was as the large as any bear that I caught while hunting in Idaho

Gary and Mary Ann Grenfell are friends of mine who live in Libby, Montana. When I first met Gary he had never hunted his dogs on bear, so one day he jumped in my truck with me and we headed to the panhandle of Idaho. It only took one hunt and he was hooked. He became a very good partner and eventually he had some pretty good bear dogs.

This photo is of Gary's wife Mary Ann, with a bear that the three of us caught in northern Idaho. This was not the last bear that either one of us caught, but it was the last bear that either Gary or I killed. After this we would simply tree them and let them go. Injuries to our dogs continued to remain the same though. Eventually, Gary had one of his dog's, Rock loose an eye while after a bear and I had a young female "Rizzie" killed outright by a very small female bear as she came down the tree.

On this hunt, Mary Ann came close to getting run over by this bear right in the middle of the fight that was settled by Gary shooting it three times with his .45 magnum, one of those shots was while it was on top of Mindy, and the last was when it had Curley down and on the ground.

*Jim Bridges. logging contractor, timber faller,
lion and bear hunter, and my friend.*

Around 2000

Jim Bridges, at his home in Susanville, CA, thirty-five years after I first started hunting with him. Jim knew how to find the big ones, and here he is with another four hundred pounder; the only thing different here was Jim was older. He still had the same strain of Walker hounds that he had from the time that I met him, and they were special. The dog on his right was named Boogie, and he came from his personal strain of Walkers. I want to point out that although Jim preferred this particular strain of Walkers, he was not what I like to call "color blind" when it came to hunting hounds. By that I mean, he could appreciate all five of the major breeds of hounds that are used to hunt for lion and bears: Walker, Bluetick, Redbone, Black and Tan, Plott, and a mixture of these. Each breed comes in different colors and they all have their own special traits and abilities. In different parts of the country one breed will seem to be more popular than others. All too often, I would find that there would be some hunters that are totally convinced that just one of these breeds was the best, and it was usually the one they are hunting. Over time, I found that there were good ones in all of these breeds and that the better ones seem to come from certain family lines and even then, not all of them actually make good hunting dogs.

Jim had a line of registered Walkers that were very impressive, and I could see why he liked them. They were definitely better than average in ability, easy to train and they were very good-looking as well. On the other hand, I was hooked on the Vaughn strain of Blueticks, but I also had other breeds. In fact, over time I had them all. It eventually became my philosophy that regardless of their color, if they were good, then they were just that: Good! In fact, my favorite saying was, "**I never saw a good dog that was the wrong color.**" Jim had the same philosophy.

Unfortunately, Jim is no longer with us,
but I can guarantee you this,
He is missed by many.

One of my best friends, and occasional hunting partner, Louis Strawn

1972

Louis Strawn and I made a trip back to Nevada in the late spring of 1972 to pick up my trailer and move it back to California. We took a drive into the Monitor Mountains. We cut this lion's track in a patch of snow where it had crossed the road we were on. From the looks of it, I believed that it had been there only a few hours earlier and he hadn't gone far from where we found his tracks, so he was an easy catch. After treeing it, I could see he was larger than average, and I decided to take him for myself. I did this, and had him mounted full size. Not the largest, but big enough. From left to right the dogs are Hammer and Tiny, both belonging to Louis, with Saylor on the right.

This lion sits in my living room today. He is mounted in a lying position.

Louis Strawn served in the Navy during WWII and survived a number of air attacks on his ship as well as the invasion of Saipan, Okinawa, and Guadalcanal. When the Japanese surrendered to General MacArthur on the USS Missouri, Louis was on a ship right beside it and was able to watch the whole thing. Not Bad!

Louis and I hunted together for many years and he kept some pretty good dogs, which he would loan to me whenever I needed them. It's not that my dogs needed help to catch bears, but when we were running and catching several bears a week, week after week, I would need to rotate the dogs so they could all get some much-needed rest.

Bull Lake, Lincoln County, Montana 1975

This photo was taken in my yard along the shores of Bull Lake in Montana. Red Farley, the gentleman on the left. He was the father of Leo Farley who I had hunted with and who killed a record-sized bear in Kern County. He was also the guy who talked me out of the Winchester lever-action rifle that I had owned since I was about twelve, for a Marlin lever-action that shot too high and I hated. He had lived somewhere around the L.A. area and also had a cabin somewhere in the Tehachapi Mountains. In 2005 I started looking for Red and Leo and after about three years I met up with a cowboy and horse farrier who told me that he had known Red, but that he had passed away. From there I started looking for friends of Leo's who were part of the archery fraternity that he had hung out with. My wife, Lynette, located Midge Dandridge who had Leo's phone number, and in late 2011, I called him and asked him about the old Winchester. Leo told me that after his dad died he had no use for it and he gave it to our friend George Wright, but if I wanted it back, he would go and get it for me. It hadn't been fired at all since I last saw it and he wanted to bring it to me. He said that in the two years before Red died, he periodically asked Leo to try and find me, that it was something he wanted before he passed away. All of this was happening at the same time I was trying to find them. But since Red passed before we could connect, what he had on his mind remains a mystery.

On January 19, 2012, Leo called to say that he was on his way up, with our friend George Wright and the Winchester. It had been forty years and three days since I had seen that old gun, and since then I have used it on two bears and one feral pig that were killing chickens, and it works just fine.

January 19, 2012
Leo & me with the old Winchester

Leo Farley, George Wright and me
Leo is holding the arrow that bounced off the bear that he killed in Bull Run in 1972
Loe gave this to me and I still have it to this day.

*Close up showing the damaged broadhead
that looked like it had hit a stonewall, instead of a bear's rib.
This is exactly the way it looked after hitting the bear.*

Chapter 20

LAST CHAPTER

In closing I want to point out that during my earliest years of hunting with hounds, I became fascinated at how a hound could trail another animal, (some of them at full speed), that had not been there for hours, and in some instances, days earlier. It was this along with their unbelievable endurance, courage, determination, and friendship that created my dedication towards them, and when it came to hunting in general, without hounds, I had no interest at all.

I cherish those memories from way back when, and mourn the untimely loss of so many wonderful hounds. I learned a lot from some of those old dogs, including a proper respect for the many animals they were trained to hunt and catch. Another thing they gave me was a trust and friendships that are rarely found in people, and it was the most difficult of all times when the day came where I had to dig a hole for their final resting place and say goodbye.

You see, they were not just dogs, or simply tools that I used and then discarded when they wore out. Most of them became part of me, and I found that the smarter ones would actually study and try to understand as much about me as they could, and I would do the same with each of them. They were my unconditional friends, and without them, I could never have done any of this. It is Bo, the one who taught me what a good dog was and showed me hundreds of times, how it was supposed to be done, that I am most thankful for. Then there was Saylor, Bo's close cousin, and the one who mentored Saylor. I realize that I haven't said much about Saylor, but he no doubt became the most talented hound that I ever owned. It is to these two, and all the others that came after them, that I am dedicating this book. After all, I was truly trained by a hound dog.

Bo, Saylor,
Thunder, Sue, Dolly,
Curley, Flipper, Spot,
Liz, Mindy, Mandy,
Sugar, Spud, Hammer,
Pat II, Rebel, Fannie, and Bonnie

ABOUT THE AUTHOR

Ed & Henry

Ed Vance, author of Trained by a Hound Dog, lives in the Southern Sierras where he started hunting as a professional guide. He and his wife Lynette live a simple life with their two Great Danes, Buckshot and Colt 45, a couple of horses, and a few mules who appeared out of nowhere. From their house he can look out across the many mountains he hunted and reminisce about some of the stories written in this book.

Visit the Author at;
www.TrainedbyaHoundDog.com